SO, SHALL THY SEED BE

DISCOVERING YOUR POSITION AND ETERNAL DESTINY

AS

A BELIEVER IN JESUS CHRIST

BY

DR. GLORIA OJUNTA

authorHOUSE

AuthorHouse™
1663 Liberty Drive
Bloomington, IN 47403
www.authorhouse.com
Phone: 833-262-8899

Published by AuthorHouse 08/05/2021

ISBN: 978-1-6655-3339-3 (sc)
ISBN: 978-1-6655-3340-9 (e)

Print information available on the last page.

Any people depicted in stock imagery provided by Getty Images are models, and such images are being used for illustrative purposes only.
Certain stock imagery © Getty Images.

This book is printed on acid-free paper.

Because of the dynamic nature of the Internet, any web addresses or links contained in this book may have changed since publication and may no longer be valid. The views expressed in this work are solely those of the author and do not necessarily reflect the views of the publisher, and the publisher hereby disclaims any responsibility for them.

All scripture quotations are from the King James Version of the bible.

CONTENTS

ACKNOWLEDGEMENTS

I'm grateful to the Lord Almighty who has inspired me to write this book. I'm also indebted to my cousin Pastor Godson Hez and my brother-in-law Professor Simon Emeje who dedicated their time to proof read and edited this book and contributed in making this book a reality.

My special thanks to my son Chinomso Ojunta who assisted in packaging and formatting this book to provide a delightful reading.

DEDICATION

To our late parents Pa Michael and Ma Violet Ekechukwu
who relentlessly committed themselves not only to provide our
physical needs for our well being and growth, but were dynamic
spiritual mentors who lived out what they thought us.

FOREWORD

So Shall Thy Seed Be

Gaining insight and revelation into any part of the Holy Bible fuels our faith in God and brings the spiritual tonic we all need to accelerate the speed of our personal spiritual growth and increase our kingdom's impact on the earth.

Dr. Gloria Ojunta has picked God's golden promise to our spiritual patriarch – Abraham, son of Terah, in Genesis 15 as a take-off point for sharing timeless truth from inception of God's restored relationship with man through Abraham and his seed to eternity.

She covers a wide variety of subjects such as our relationship with God as a special gift, the significance of the seed, the importance of our choice of excellent soil to plant the seed, and the glorious harvest that follows if we do it right.

She relates this 'seed' to the choice of a life partner in marriage and blessedness of bonding properly together, soul and body. You will find it interesting reading.

Professor Mosy U. Madugba

INTRODUCTION

The promise of God to Abraham that his Seed would be like the stars of Heaven has often been misinterpreted or misrepresented by some religious folks. They think that God was referring to the numerical counts of people which turned out to be the people of Israel today.

This book will widen your scope of knowledge and reframe the minds of so many beliefs concerning God's stand in His promise to Abraham. Abraham saw the promise afar, embraced the promise, was persuaded of it, yet he died in faith without receiving it (Heb. 11:11-13). "Abraham offered up Isaac and he that received the promise offered his only begotten son" (Heb 11:17). The offering of Isaac was to affirm the fulfillment of the promise many years after the exit of Abraham. We need a good understanding of this innumerable seed as they occupy a serious position in God's covenant program. We are of this Seed. God's expectation to fulfillment of this promise in us relates to the faith that Abraham manifested. This same faith is in us as believers. This promise is fulfilled in us, the believers, after the exit

CHAPTER 1

God's Promise to Abraham

God's promise to Abraham is wrapped up in being the reward first, before rewarding Abraham for his faithfulness. When God becomes a reward to you, he pours out his love in your heart. This love subjects you to remain faithful to him. This faithfulness breathes out his eternal reward on you.

"I am thy shield and thy exceedingly great reward . . . Look now towards heaven, and tell the stars, if thou be able to number them: So shall thy seed be" (Gen. 15:1, 5).

God told Abraham that **He is** his reward. The promise was not what was about to come, but what God meant to Abraham at the time of promise. God never promised Abraham that '**He will be his reward**'. It was not a promise that is yet to come, but a profound statement of who God is to Abraham. God's promise is wrapped up in who He becomes to you at the time you truly repent and accept Him.

This promise came "after these things" (Gen 15:1). God's promise to Abraham was made after Abraham's unselfish move. This was after Abraham gave Melchizedek the tithes of all the spoil he received from the slaughter of Chedorlamor (Gen. 14:17-24). Abraham's unselfish move caught God's attention. Also, only when God Himself becomes Abraham's reward would Abraham's seed be as the stars of the heaven. Abraham's reward was God Himself coming in the flesh. "Now to Abraham and his seed were the promises made. He saith not, and to seeds, as of many but as of one, and to thy seed, which is Christ" (Gal. 3:16). The promises were made to Abraham and to 'a Seed' and not to seeds of Abraham.

God requested Abraham to number the stars (Gen15:5). Is God referring to the numerical count of the stars, the descriptive nature of the stars, or both? "That in blessing I will bless thee, and in multiplying I will multiply thy seed as the stars of the heavens and as the sand of the sea shore and thy seed shall possess the gates of your enemies, And in thy seed shall all the nations of the earth be blessed" (Gen. 22:17-18).

The promise refers to the descriptive nature of the Seed and not necessarily the numerical counts of seeds. The Seed shall be a blessing to all nations of the earth and "possess the gates of your enemies". This is not to say that the Seed will be multiplied to produce many other Seeds. In other words, God was not referring to reproduction of many Christs on earth. It is only the Seed that will possess the gates of your enemies and not many Seeds. God is not referring to many Seeds, but to a particular Seed. The comparison of Abraham's Seed with the countless number of stars, evidently describes the nature and mission of the Seed; "So shall thy seed be." Your Seed shall be as countless as the stars.

SIGNIFICANCE OF THE SEED

One may want to know how this Seed relates to the numbering of the stars of heaven. Just as the stars cannot be quantified, so the Seed cannot be numbered. Stars are many, but the Seed is one and yet this Seed cannot be numbered. How can one Seed be multiplied as the stars of heaven and yet cannot be numbered? The answer is simply stated in the book of John. "Except a corn of wheat falls and dies, it abideth alone" (John 12:24). The only way the Seed will multiply is through the death of the Seed. It is, therefore, definite to state categorically and clearly that God was not referring to the reproduction of many other Christs coming in the form of men, but a reproduction of God's nature in man through the death of his only begotten son Jesus Christ.

God does not only refer to the number of stars in heaven, but He also refers to the beauty and His glory. God told Abraham first to "tell" the stars. To tell the stars could logically mean to describe the nature of the stars. If Abraham can describe the magnitude of beauty, glory and identity within the stars, then he will be able to describe the extent of God's nature in this Seed. Can you tell the stars? Can you describe the magnitude of God's glory in the stars? Even the scientists cannot come up with this.

"Every star differs in glory" (1Cor. 15:42). All stars have the same identity, but the positioning, sockets, and directions of reflection of their lights differ from star to star. "Every star has a name" (Ps. 147:4). "Each star stays in its socket from generation to generation, and each star is identified by the greatness of His power" (Is 40:26). The splendor, measure of greatness, and power in Abraham's seed cannot be quantified. This Seed is unlimited in authority and dominion. His kingdom is eternal: God rules over the heavens and the earth, just as the stars occupy the vast heavens in their specific glory and splendor. The stars have their authorities registered over the vast of clouds. The righteous in Christ shall rule over the earth because of the authority in Christ.

NATURE OF THE SEED

What is the nature of this promised seed? What did God have in mind at the promise? The nature, the number, the identity of your seed would be as the stars of heaven. Let us, therefore, examine this promised seed in Christ Jesus as revealed in Gal. 3:16. God used the stars as the descriptive expression of intensity and magnitude of Abraham's reward. Therefore, we will consider the vast nature, intensity, dominion, immortality, and indestructibility of the Seed as compared with the star.

We will also look at the nature and significance of this seed in man and as the seed relates to God and eternity.

A study of the nature of the star revealed in the Holy Bible will give you an expansive understanding of the magnitude of Abraham's reward in the promised seed. Obviously, the star should not be worshipped. Only the creator should be worshipped.

God needed Abraham to have a concrete revelation of who He is in dominion and might through the coming Seed (the Messiah). Therefore, God used concrete images that Abraham could understand, like the stars and the sands of the sea, with which to compare the infinite might of the Messiah. We should not forget that God is omnipresent. Although God is invisible, He becomes visible through the things that He made (Rom. 1:20). Therefore, to study this invisible Seed, we will be taking a critical look at the visible stars. We will also reflect on the nature of this Seed and discover how to make this eternal Seed visible through our faith.

When we make God our reward, God's word becomes flesh inside of us, just like the word became flesh inside Mary's womb. God's promise is not what is yet to come, but what He is to us as we embrace His love now. He is our Redeemer in Christ, the beginning and the end of our faith, author of our eternal salvation and destiny, to mention but a few (Rev 1:9, Heb 5:9, John 3:16). Abraham's reward for embracing God's love was eternity. God is eternal, Abraham's seed is eternal. "God so loved the world that he gave his only begotten son that whosoever believes in Him should not perish, but have eternal life" (John 3:16). Eternity is Christ in us. What then is eternal life or eternity? "So shall thy seed be."

CHAPTER 2

The Seed is Eternal Life

Just as the stars are eternal, so shall this Seed be. The Seed shall be eternal, a life that never dies. What is the significance of the word, eternal? This eternal signifies indestructible life. It is the life and nature of God. The Bible describes eternal life as the knowledge of God. "This is eternal life, that they might know thee..." (John 17:3). We are partakers of this nature through our knowledge in Christ Jesus (2 Pet. 1:3-4). As we partake and walk daily in this indestructible, immortal nature and victorious life in Christ Jesus, through faith in his word, the Seed is multiplied in us. Eternity is revelation of God in man through the promised Seed Christ. "But whoever drinketh the water I shall give Him, shall never thirst, but the water I shall give Him shall be in Him a well of water springing up to everlasting life" (John 4:14).

Stars are indestructible. The stars remain constant in the clouds. They never change positions and remain ever glorious. Therefore, the Seed will be as indestructible and unchanging as the stars. Just as God revealed Himself to Abraham in his promised seed, so He also reveals Himself to us in his Seed, Christ Jesus, who is the express image of the Father and the brightness of his glory (Heb 1:3). "If you see me, you have seen the father" (John 14:9). "I can of mine own self do nothing, as I hear, I judge: and my judgment is just because I seek not mine own will, but the will of the father which hath sent me" (John 5:30). "This is life eternal, that they might know thee, the only true God, and Jesus Christ whom thou hast sent" (John 17:3).

He is the God of then and now. God does not change. He remains the same for all eternity. Eternal life is who God is to you now. Who do you say He is? The Lord is not only known for His acts, but also in his principles? How has God revealed Himself to you? This revelation is indestructible and eternal. Many people only see eternity as life after death. Such people believe eternity does not begin until after the spirit exits the body. Eternity truly begins when you accept Jesus into your life. The salvation of your soul is your entrance into eternity as long as you remain faithful to Jesus (Heb 3:6). Since eternity begins with a new birth in Christ, the new life becomes an offspring of life after death. What God is to you now is what he is after death. God remains constant not only for you but also for generations after you. He is our eternal reward in Christ.

PURPOSE OF SALVATION

The main purpose of salvation is not only to attain Heaven, but also to share our knowledge of God with the next generation. A life eternal is a life that continues beyond the grave when our spirits exit this earthly body to be present with the Lord. "The memory of the righteous is blessed: but the name of the wicked shall rot," (Prov 10:7). We need to seek and fully experience God while here on earth. To experience Him is to experience his righteousness, love, peace, and power. With God in our lives, we can live in health, in abundance, and in freedom. We can walk in love, without fear, resentment, jealousy, or anger toward each other. Consequently, living a holy life acceptable to Him, we will feel good about ourselves and about others. To experience God means to experience His presence. As His will is in heaven, so it is on the earth (Luke 11:2). As He is, so are we. His presence gives the divine enablement, which is the anointing to live above the natural and to keep away from sin and reproach.

Our freedom in Christ does not mean that we should satisfy the desires of our flesh and live recklessly. We cannot hold unto His grace to forgive us our sins while we continue to commit those sins. "Whosoever is born of God sinneth not" (1John 5:18). "Shall we remain in sin that grace may abound? God forbid. How shall we that are dead to sin, live any longer therein?" (Rom 6:1-2). Consequently, having Christ in our lives does not mean we are free to sin. Instead, we are free from sin through his grace. The availability of his grace is the enabling power to live above sin. Our freedom in Him energizes us to live an uncompromising life of faith. Therefore, our faith in God allows us to live above sin, resisting the suggestions of the devil. His abiding grace provides us with this arm of strength. We must depend on His grace to live above unrighteousness. "Walk in the Spirit, and you will not fulfill the lust of the flesh" (Gal. 5:16).

The only way to live above these desires is to walk in His presence. His presence will elude such temptations. We must direct our thirst and hunger away from temptations of the flesh and redirect our thirst and hunger to please Him daily by living according to his expectations. This redirection begins our eternity, even while we are on Earth. Faith in God is more than believing that God will grant us our material requests. Having faith in God also means believing that His redeeming grace will grant us a holy and righteous life before Him.

When persecuted, God grants us grace to rejoice and remain peaceful, When we are despised by sinners, for living righteously, denying worldly pleasures because of our faith and belief. God gives us grace to forgive our offenders and to live above fleshly desires. "Blessed are they who are persecuted for righteousness sake for theirs is the kingdom of God. Blessed are ye when men shall revile you and persecute you and shall say all manner of evil against you falsely for my sake. Rejoice and be exceedingly glad for great is your reward in heaven" (Matt. 5:10-12). The pursuit of righteousness is difficult and foolish to the natural mind, but attaining righteousness will rain down many blessings.

BEGINNING OF ETERNAL LIFE

This pursuit is the beginning of eternity. "Seek ye first the kingdom of God and his righteousness and every other thing will be added to you" (Luke 12:31). The kingdom of God is righteousness, peace and joy in the Holy Ghost (Rom14:17). These are the identities of the Kingdom. Maintaining peace and joy in Christ in tribulations and at all times is the kingdom principle. When our souls which are the seats of our emotions are prospering in these three distinct ingredients of the kingdom, then we will remain eternally successful. Righteousness is not just right standing with God, but also the right standing in God. One might stand with him but not necessarily stand in him. Standing in him is seen in manifestation of his boldness and authority towards the attack and suggestions of the devil. "The righteousness of God is revealed from faith to faith and the righteous shall live by faith" (Rom 1:17). God's righteousness is seen in the faith of Jesus Christ (Rom 3: 2) and is a gift from God.

Eternity is not granted once we reach heaven. Eternity is God's reward to us when we accept Christ into our hearts. Eternity is the sufficiency of His grace to stay in his presence and withstand the suggestions of the Devil, simply called temptations. God is omnipresent. He created heaven and resides in heaven. Heaven is his creation. God's throne and house are in heaven. Heaven is his seat of authority. The White House is where all the decisions and policies are made to keep the United States of America running. It is the seat of government and the house of the President. "Heaven is my throne and earth is my footstool. Where is the house that you build for me? Where is my place of rest?" (Isaiah 66:1).

God's throne is in heaven, and he expects heaven on earth. We are God's throne on earth. This is why he demands his house (throne) in us.

We feel God's presence during our fellowship with Him. Our fellowship with God is where and when transformation of our lives take place. Therefore, our spirits become God's house. Our spirit with God is eternal. The spirit of a saved soul goes to God when he exits the body. Wherever God is, the spirit is also. "The tabernacle of God is with men, and He will dwell with them, and they shall be his people, and God Himself shall be with them, and be their God" (Rev. 21:3).

Therefore, we must realize that the pressures of this life are avenues of knowing Him intimately. Difficulties and hardships on earth create a strong wall of fellowship and communion with Him. We live eternally as we allow Him to use these pressures to build eternity (2 Cor. 4:16-18). We live eternally as we allow these pressures to burn off fleshly desires and demolish pride, creating avenues of love and patience within us. These pressures are avenues of solidifying his throne in us. This is the ministry of reconciliation. Reconciliation is our daily work with God to renew our minds. As His words, principles, and ways continuously renew our minds, we will become more like Him. This makes us the throne of God. "Our afflictions are temporal and work eternal weight of glory" (2 Cor. 4:17).

This "eternal weight of glory" means that the storms of life are for eternal recommendation. The storms remind us to keep our eternity forever in our thoughts and actions. The result of faith and trust in the Lord can never be eradicated. Even when we do not remember, God keeps a record of our faith. Thus, the way we live our lives can affect the generations that follow us; this stimulates generational blessings for the next generation, even after our transition into glory.

This weight is life eternal, even as "the stars of the heavens" are eternal. "Our suffering of this present time is nothing compared with

9

the glory which shall be revealed in us. For the earnest expectation of the creature waiteth for the manifestation of the sons of God. For the creature itself also **shall** be delivered from the bondage of corruption into the glorious liberty of the children of God" (Rom. 8:18-21). The word "**shall**" connotes a future event. Once we are saved, our purpose in life should be to seek the deliverance of the creature (the upcoming generation) through the manifestations in spirit of loyalty, love, patience, and faith. These legacies of eternity will be left behind us for the generations to come. The creature is not waiting for the sons of God, but manifestations of the power of son-ship; which is Christ in us manifesting on the outside.

Jesus is a manifestation of God's power, nature, faith, hope, love, and blessing. We are not in the world to accumulate riches to heal sickness in our old age, nor are we here to accumulate a debt of sins and reproaches for future generations to reap. Instead, we are here to ensure eternal freedom for our generations. We are here to seek eternal treasures and to build empires of good works of love and faith for generations to reap. Many of us reap the eternal rewards left behind by past generations.

The Bible is the revelation of experiences with God. Through the Bible, God reveals corrections, examples, and teachings. The Bible is an eternal reward given to us by the past giants of faith. The revelation of Him in the time of suffering is eternity. This imperishable treasure is hidden in the earthen vessel (2 Cor. 4:7). As new creatures, we become God's pulpit on Earth. "So shall thy seed be, as the stars of the heavens" (Gen. 15:5). We become imperishable treasures of generations. We become an ark of everlasting freedom. "My sheep hear my voice and they follow me, and I give them eternal life and they shall not perish, neither shall any man pluck them out of my hand" (John 10:27-28). Hearing God's voice is a condition for possessing eternal life and for remaining indestructible. Any time we pass through a storm and come out clean and unharmed, God commends eternity.

CHAPTER 3

The Indestructible Love

The love of this Seed cannot be destroyed just like the stars remain indestructible. As the stars remain indestructible, the love in us as God's children is indestructible. Nothing can separate us from the love of God. It is an indestructible love (Rom. 8:38). God's love is unconditional and unchanging agape love. Not even sin can stand between God and us. We are "troubled on every side, yet not distressed" (2 Cor. 4:8), because of the indestructible seed inside us. His plans and purposes for our lives are indestructible. This is why our souls remain indestructible in every challenges of life. He is our great reward as we remain committed and obedient like Abraham.

Although the stars seem to move when we look at them through the clouds, they stay in the same position relative to one another. Neither weather conditions nor seasonal changes, caused by the tilting of the earth's axis, affects the positions of the stars. Circumstances around us will not move away God's love for us. The Seed within us remains to transform our lives as He shines on us. However, our values change as we embrace his love to live a rich and spiritual life. He is the same yesterday, today, and forever. As we recognize this abiding love, we are daily transformed to his image. This places us in a position to be able to recognize his voice and not just his word.

VOICE OF THE SEED

Many Christians identify his word and not his voice. Quite often we use these two interchangeably, and the enemy has deceived many with this. The word of God goes with his voice and his voice is identified in His love. We should not forget that the temptations of the Devil on Christ were solidly backed up with the word of God. (Luke 4:3,6,10). It is important, therefore, to note that Jesus committed himself to us as the Shepherd over his sheep, and the sheep must be able to hear his word expressed by his voice. This is because the only thing that can attract the sheep to the shepherd and brings loyalty and submission to the voice of the Shepherd is Love. "And when he putteth forth his own sheep, he goeth before them, and the sheep follow him for they know his voice. As the Father knoweth me, even so know I the Father and I lay down my life for the sheep" (John 10:4,15). It is not all the words of God that come from his voice.

The Devil came to Jesus with words of His Father, but Christ defied this authority, because it was not the voice of his Father. The voice was not born out of love, concern and passion, but out of selfish intents. If these words had come directly from God the Father, Jesus would have obeyed. As we approach the second advent of Christ, discernment of the spirit speaking to us even in our churches, relationship and any where we are, is very important. The Devil has actually sneaked into marriages, churches, schools, government officials, televisions, radios, to speak the word which is not necessarily God's voice. These words come with selfish motives to deceive even the believers. "Beloved, believe not every spirit, but try the spirits whether they are of God: because many false prophets are gone out into the world. We are of God: he that knoweth God heareth us; he that is not of God heareth not us. Hereby know we the spirit of truth, and the spirit of error" (1John 4:1,6).

How did Christ discern the satanic approach to him? All the tempting words came with selfish motives. Devil did not tempt Him to do things that directly contradicted the law of God, like stealing, committing adultery. He rather, tried to entice Jesus with material gains:

bread, riches, and affluence. Though he quoted from the words of God, Jesus discerned the voice of the devil behind the words. So shall thy seed be. By reason of the seed, you will be able to recognize and follow His voice through His indestructible agape love and passion for you. What a mystery?

CHAPTER 4

The Seed: A Permanent Testimony

Testimonies that are connected with the seed are permanent. For example, Sarah's testimony of God is permanent. She judged God faithful (Heb. 11:11). Do we judge God faithful, righteous, merciful, and patient in our circumstances? *WHO DO WE SAY HE IS?* How we judge God becomes a legacy for generations, both born and unborn. These testimonies will remain and spread out over the surface of the Earth as the waters cover the sea. "We overcome the devil by the words of our testimonies" (Rev. 12:11); from one generation to another generation. Our future generations will overcome the devil by using the same words of our testimonies.

LIVING TESTIMONIES

Testimonies are not necessarily the manifestations of expected results. Instead, effective testimonies are a result of how much of Him we get to know during the period of waiting and how much of our knowledge of Him we share with others. How we judge Him in every situation of our lives determines the testimonies. However, He gives us grace to judge Him rightly. We are expected not only to share these testimonies, but also to live them for others to see; for example, whenever we judge Him faithful, He expects us to be faithful to Him and to others. Not only are we called to witness, but we are also called to be living witnesses. We can only witness what we have seen and heard (Acts 1:8). Furthermore, we can only witness what we are living. We are expected to be living witnesses.

The effectiveness of our witnesses is seen in our daily lives and not in what we say. So shall thy seed be; a living testimonies for generations and not just preaching testimonies. Our salvation is loud to the sight of men by our daily lives and walk with God, rather than what we say. This should be a true and real test of our standing faith in Christ. Our faith in action is seen in our works rather than in what we say. The stars are obvious in the skies. The same way, we are visible and testify to the glory of God by our daily assignments and respective activities. These activities remain imperishable. Salvation is unto good works. This is eternity, and imperishable, standing steadfast, unshakable and refusing to compromise with the onslaughts, tricks and gimmicks of the devil. "So shall thy seed be."

How much empowerment and anointing will be instilled in us during our lives? How much of His principles and wisdom will we receive? How faithful and obedient will we be? How well will we keep His commandments and statutes without compromise, in spite of the storms of life or trials and unexpected tragedies? How much of His nature will be revealed and work inside of us? Only through the help of the Holy Spirit can we achieve these things. God is the One who measures and keeps eternal record of our progress. The seed is eternal.

We need to focus our interest on understanding his ways, principles, and methods of approach, as we experience His miracles. He is not only the God of miracles; He is also the God of wonders in His sovereign nature. God expects us not only to know His personality, but also His principles. Therefore, He guides us to understand situations and judge situations according to His understanding. We should not be quick in reacting to issues, but should seek first an understanding from the Lord to guide us in the best manner.

Many times, we hasten to pray and make requests that contradict God's views and understanding concerning certain issues. We allow our emotions to carry the prayers to God instead of allowing God to send us His will. If we will remain quiet and calm while we seek His guidance, we will stand a far better chance of hearing God. The God of principles is holy and perfect in all ways.

"In all thy ways, acknowledge Him and he will direct your paths" (Prov. 3:6). Acknowledging His ways and principles of operations opens doors for great victories. Following God's principles gives us an insight of what His thoughts are concerning every issue and guides us to pray correctly and sincerely.

ETERNAL PERCEPTIONS AND VIEWS

Learning how to follow God's principles and how to pray correctly are part of our eternity. "So shall thy seed be." He showed Moses His ways, and He showed the people of Israel His acts (Ps. 103:7). We should not focus on just receiving results, but we should have our victories more on revelation of His wisdom, manner of seeing and approaching issues. Furthermore, we should learn to judge Him based on the wealth of knowledge revealed to our spirits by the Holy Spirit. This is life eternal.

We can best learn how to judge God by studying a few women and men of faith in the Bible. By judging the Lord faithful, Sarah received strength to conceive seed and deliver a child at old age (Heb. 11:11). Furthermore, Abraham considered neither the deadness of Sarah's womb nor the deadness of his body as hindrances to God's commitment to his word. In addition, he did not consider the killing of Isaac a hindrance to God's faithfulness (Rom. 4:18-20). Against all hopes, God gave hope. Abraham knew God gives and takes life. He saw God's wisdom despite the detestable situations. Abraham saw Him as the God of impossibilities who demonstrates His power when we believe Him enough to perform the impossible. Consequently, Abraham demonstrated the nature of God in his faith. A sacrificial offering to God attracts his sacrificial responsibility to man. Abraham understood the basic requirements of faith. He knew that faith required not only the mystery of confession, but also an act of obedience.

David received true revelations of God in all his afflictions and expressed them in the book of Psalms for our growth. David saw Him as a God who never despises a humble and a contrite heart. We should not fear to ask God for forgiveness, for God has an everlasting mercy and desires to work with repentant hearts. David knew that righteousness, uprightness, and integrity are the keys that unlock God's blessings. David delved more into the heart of God than he did into His hands. He understood that the free entrance to His divine assistance and favor was to seek his heart. Furthermore, He understood that this was the easiest and fundamental way of staying in His presence. David also understood that praise and worship are the salt of loyalty and covenant that passes into God's heart. David expresses these understandings in the book of psalms for generations to reap. They are eternal expressions of knowledge and principles of God.

Peter identified Him through the Holy Spirit as the "Christ, the son of the living God" (Matt. 16:16). This new identity changed his name from Simon Barjona to Simon Peter. "Upon this rock will I build my church and the gates of hell will not prevail" (Matt. 16:18). Upon this revealed identity is the church built. Freedom and empowerment are in the revealed knowledge hidden inside of us. The chains on Peter's hands fell off at the words "arise up quickly" (Acts 12:7), because the revelation inside Peter with this word from the angel destroyed the chain and brought freedom to Peter.

In the book of Daniel, Daniel judged God faithful when he faced threats from the Babylonian king, Nebuchadnezzar (Dan. 2:19-23).

Daniel's promotion and enlightenment of his gift was at the decree of the wicked king. Daniel stood firm in what he believed and refused to be intimidated by human threats. He understood that such boldness attracts God's presence, favor, and assistance. Because of the encounter with the wicked king, Daniel's knowledge of God increased. The decree of the unrighteous is always for the promotion and elevation of the righteous.

Solomon demonstrates his wisdom in Proverbs, Ecclesiastes, and the Songs of Solomon. Solomon understood that riches and wealth are in God's wisdom. He sought wisdom more than he sought material wealth. Therefore, God garnished Solomon with royalty and honor. Habakkuk and many other prophets of God did likewise.

During His entire ministry on Earth, Jesus did not only experience results in his prayers to his Father, but He also judged God in view of his relationship and revealed truth. The synoptic gospels declare Jesus' ministry. Understanding His mission, Jesus focused on His objective and completed the assignment. He understood his divine assignment and accomplished it, irrespective of the challenges and the confrontations from the laymen. Jesus wished to please his Father. The Bible presents us with the supreme example of faithfulness to God through Jesus. Jesus learned obedience through his sufferings, stooped to conquer death, and tapped resurrection power from his Father. He exhibited great willingness to please his Father for the redemption of man, Jesus obeyed God.

In the Bible, many more people of faith provide excellent examples of their obedience to God: Job, Esther, Ruth, and Samson are few of the faith giants. They lived their lives to receive eternal commendations. The revelations they all had in God are recorded in the Holy Bible and linger from eternity to eternity. "So shall thy seed be." Their lives became eternal testimonies, and the record of their testimonies in the

Bible became a guide for all generations. We must not let our generations carry burdens that God did not put on them. Instead, we must let the seed inside us be the eternal light that will lead them out of the darkness. As children of God, we are His eternity on Earth.

CHAPTER 5

God: Our Eternity

God is our eternity. Our intimacy with Him starts while we are on Earth so that we will not be strangers to Him at the time of our transition. Moses, at the burning bush, asked God to introduce Himself. God called Moses by his name, yet Moses needed to know who was sending him to Egypt (Ex. 3:13-15). God introduced Himself as an eternal God, transmitting His goodness through families from generation to generation. "He is the God of Abraham, Isaac, and Jacob."

Christ's success in his ministry was deep rooted and grounded in intimate knowledge of his Father. "He did not think it robbery to be equal to God but made Himself of no reputation and took the form of a servant, and was made the likeness of men" (Phil. 2:6-7). This gave Him victory over death. The Seed understood who He was and through the unrighteous decree of Pontius Pilate and his Jewish associates, He was exalted above measure. He recognized his position with God, yet He willingly became flesh so that He might save us. Today, we are enjoying that freedom in Christ through the power of the Holy Spirit. Each new generation continuously enjoys this freedom. This is our eternity. Such freedom should humble us and not make us proud.

Moreover, we must understand that Christ came also to be our example. Therefore, such humility in Him should create inward humility in us for subsequent victories. For us and for generations ahead, this is eternal life. As we build our revelations of His splendor, our knowledge of Him brings us a long lasting empowerment of trust and obedience in Him. As we tarry from generation to generation, we should always focus our interest on God during every storm. At times, when we are faced with storms of life, we forget our previous victories. This does not conform to the eternal example. Every victory and huddle passed should be in everlasting remembrance. God commanded Joshua to lay stones in the middle of the Jordan River after passing the river. These stones rest as memorial to this day (Josh. 4:9). We are eternal epistles of God to our generation and the generations to come. We should be able to leave the legacies of God's power and witnesses to generations to come. "As the stars of the heavens . . . so shall thy seed be".

THE BIBLE IS ETERNAL SEED

The Bible is the legacy left for our instruction, correction and growth through the teaching ministry of the Holy Spirit, using committed men and women of God. "So shall thy seed be as the stars of heaven." Our Seed shall be an eternal record for salvation and deliverance for many. Our Seed shall be recorded in man and eternity for many. He shall witness and be a witness for many. The Bible is a revelation of eternity. The Bible is the eternal institute of God's glory and power. Once more, "all creatures are waiting for the manifestations of this glory and power in you, because the creature itself also shall be delivered from the bondage of corruption into the glorious liberty of the children of God" through your witnesses of who He is (Rom. 8:19-21). Therefore, we are the eternal hope of God, as we live His word through the Seed inside of us.

CHAPTER 6

The Mission of the Seed

The mission of the seed can easily be seen at the grave of Lazarus. The same Mary that anointed Jesus feet invited Jesus to come and heal Lazarus. Jesus did not turn up to heal, because he needed to demonstrate the final purpose of his mission on earth. He was not only a healing Messiah, but the resurrection and life. (John 11:6-7).

"Jesus wept" (John 11:35). The weeping of the seed brought many sons and daughters into glory, just like the stars over the vast heavens. The Seed saw the rejections, sin and reproach of man; He saw the sting of death, and wept with passion. "So shall thy seed be." If thou had known even thou at least in this thy day, the things which belong unto thy peace, but now they are hidden from thine eyes. For the days shall come upon thee, that thine enemies shall cast a trench about thee and compass thee round, and keep thee in on every side (Luke 19:42). Your weeping, born of compassion for salvation of souls, can release the anger of God against satanic bondage over their souls. "Labor not for the meat that perisheth but for that which endures unto everlasting life" (John 6:27). "The harvest is plenteous, but laborers are few. Pray ye, therefore, the Lord of harvest that He might send laborers into the harvest" (Matt. 9:38). Your labor can be seen in your weeping for conversion of souls.

This weeping from the Lord, released immense anger from the Lord to call Lazarus back to life, breaking the chains and captivity of death. God's indignation was released. The pangs of death were actually destroyed at Lazarus' grave when "Jesus cried with a loud voice: Lazarus come forth" (John 11:43). This energized the faith of Christ to the cross.

The destruction of death at the tomb of Lazarus was an assurance of hope for Christ.

"For the joy that was set before him, he endured the cross" (Heb. 12:2). With great joy, Christ had received the victory over death before He went to the cross. The assignment was completed before His death. The tomb was empty, because the stone was rolled away not by Him but by His word. He knew that in the same way, the stone would be rolled away at his grave. An angel sat on the stone to avoid the rolling back of the stone to cover the grave. If the stone had not been rolled away, there would not have been an exit from the grave. Jesus saw the stone rolled away at his own grave, too. Therefore, He stood firm in that joy and with boldness, faced death without fear, trembling, or intimidation. Instead, Jesus faced death with love, joy, courage, and simplicity of mind. He was ready to defy the shame to which He would be submitted because of the expected victory and triumph. Fear comes when victory is not seen before the storm.

AT THE TOMB

I have often wondered in my heart why a Christian should fear pressures. Nothing takes a saved soul unaware; just as death did not take Christ unaware. Therefore, a Christian is expected to be aware of approaching storms, because he/she should have a prior revelation of the intents and victory. This should be the joy set before you. No trial comes without an accompanying and completed victory. We cannot be tempted beyond that which we have already won. The tomb is always empty before we face any trial. Likewise, the tomb was empty before the cross. The Seed saw the empty tomb before He faced death. This encouraged Him and set a fullness of joy before His destiny. In the same manner, every believer and blood-bought child of God should not in any way fear the trials, but should like Jesus, see the emptiness of the tomb before the trials. Therefore, the empty tomb is the symbol of Christianity, because the empty tomb overtook the cross

The Seed declared His mission at the tomb. He did not meet Lazarus when Lazarus was sick because the sickness was not unto death (John 11:4). The sickness was merely a tool used for the eternal destiny of man. Lazarus illness was a stepping-stone to the rolling away of all limitations and a stepping-stone to the emptiness of the tomb. "So shall thy seed be." The Seed inside of you declared His victory when the situation was at its worst and most hopeless moment. Although Jesus could have saved Lazarus from dying by going earlier to heal him, but the Seed allowed him to die and become a corpse, as a testimony of His coming resurrection. "So shall thy seed be", a testimony of resurrection from every hopeless situation; Halleluya!

CHAPTER 7

Significance of Weeping

A number of people have seen tears in times of tribulations as signs of weaknesses and unbelief. To this set of people, a renewal of minds and understanding will establish the faith in tears.

There are four kinds of tears:

--Tears of passion and love.

--Tears of joy, trust, and faith.

--Tears for judgment against satanic oppression.

--Tears of sorrow, self-pity, fear, and unbelief.

PASSION AND LOVE

The tears at Lazarus' tomb were tears of passion, love, and concern for humanity. These tears released the spirit of indignation that cried and called Lazarus to life (John 11:43). The voice that called Lazarus from death was not just a natural voice, but also the voice of indignation against sin and death. Therefore, God releases a dimension of faith that accompanies the motive of our cries to Him.

Tears that are spirit motivated with passion and sincerity attract the indignation of God to destroy the onslaught of the devil. Jesus cried on the cross with passion, and strength came upon Him. Remember that the word of God must always be carried by a specific voice. His voice carries the mission that it is sent out to do. Adam heard the Voice walking in the garden, and hid himself in the garden. (Gen. 3:8). The voice came to search out Adam. Sin could not tolerate the Voice. Adam heard the voice and hid himself (Gen 3:8).

27

Furthermore, God interprets the voice of your cries to Him in a way that only the Spirit of God can understand. Consequently, God acts according to the interpretations He receives (Rom 8:26).

TEARS OF LOVE, TRUST AND FAITH

So our voices can be heard in our tears and God interprets these voices. The tears of the blind Bartimaeus attracted Jesus. The Lord stood still, being touched by the feelings (Mk 10:47-49). The motive of that cry brought Jesus' attention to Bartimaeus. The motive that touched Jesus was that of trust and assurance with an expectation. The man never saw Jesus; he only heard Jesus coming his way. Likewise, our tears can be an expression of our love and faith.

The sinner who approached Jesus washed the master's feet with her tears. The expression of her faith and love was seen in those tears. The Lord highly recommended her faith (Luke 7:37-38). These tears were of faith and passion for the Lord. Many times when you express the thoughts of your heart through the streaming tears of your soul, the Lord sees through the tears and visits you in an awesome manner. We should always remember that the soul is the seat of our emotions and feelings, and we have a High Priest who is touched by the feelings of our infirmities. The inability to express ourselves in words but in tears can be an infirmity; thus, Christ is touched by such feelings, because our feelings are connected to our souls.

Man's soul is the Lord's breath. "And the Lord God formed man of the dust of the ground and breathed into his nostrils the breath of life and man became a living soul" (Gen. 2:7). The soul of man, which is the breath of God, is the seat of man's will, purpose, and emotions. This means that the cry of the righteous One is a release of His emotions. Coming from His soul, the cries become the breath of life. The release of life touches life (God). "The eyes of the Lord are upon the righteous and his ears are open to their cry (Ps. 34:15). The righteous cry, and the Lord heareth and delivered them out of all their troubles" (Ps. 34:15-17).

TEARS FOR JUDGEMENT AGAINST SATANIC OPPRESSIONS

"My cry came before him even into his ears, then the earth shook and trembled, the foundation of the hills also was moved and shaken because he was wrath. There went up a smoke out of his nostrils and fire out of his mouth devoured coals. Coals were kindled by it. He bowed the heavens also, and came down and darkness was under his feet" (Ps. 18:7-9). Your cry releases the indignation of God with fire that consumes the oppressions of the devil, destroys and devours the powers of darkness.

The Hebrew word for soul is PSUCHE, meaning breath! The soul is the breath of life. Man was made a living soul through the breath of life (Gen2:7). The Seed shall be touched by our feelings and feelings are expressions of our emotions. The soul is the seat of our emotions. He will declare his dominion and victory over sin, struggles, and oppressions through the tears of the saved soul. These tears release smokes of fire out of the breath. "So shall thy seed be": Tears streaming out with compassion, love, and concern for the dying world.

TEARS OF SORROW, SELF-PITY, FEAR, AND UNBELIEF.

We must however observe at this juncture that every tear of sorrow, arising from self-pity, fear of the unknown, unbelief, bitterness, jealousy, envy, comparative and competitive tears, and other fleshly instigated tears do not touch him, because these tears do not come from the breath of God. These tears are sensual and not entreating God's love. Even tears of bereavement must be faithfully motivated for God to rain down His mercies.

CHAPTER 8

The Seed is the Light

No one sees the stars in daylight. As long as there is still a glimpse of daylight, the star hides itself and shines in thick cloud of darkness. The stars are only visible to the eyes in thick cloud of darkness. Even with the height of the stars, their light still shines for as long as it is dark. In the same way, God knows the deep things of darkness. Nothing takes him unawares. Even when it seems He is far from us, he still comes as twilight in darkness. Though silent, but visibly mighty in our battles.

He is the light; He shines brighter and brighter in the thick, dark clouds of our life. Though Eliphaz accused Job of sin in the Book of Job, yet he gave a correct description of God's presence in darkness as compared with the stars. "Is not God in the height of heaven? And behold the height of the stars, how high they are! And thou sayest, "How doth God know? Can he judge through the dark cloud?" (Job 22:12-13). The height of stars is insignificant in the manifestation of their lights. "So shall thy seed be."

The Seed is the light of the world that shines through the darkness, no matter how far away he seems to be in your trying moments. "He makes darkness his secret place" (Ps. 18:11). He judges through the dark clouds of your misery, because that is his seat of office. This secret place will be discussed later in this book. The light exposes darkness. Many times, we do not know what to ask for in our darkest moment. However, the light of His word (seed) inside of us can burst open the secret of the problem, and the power of the anointing destroys the bondage.

Nothing is visible in a darkroom. Not until you switch on the light will you then see the position of every article in the room. In the same manner, the light inside of you will expose the area that needs intercessions and supplications before the Lord. This is the purpose of salvation and the difference between a saved and an unsaved soul. The saved soul sees as the Seed sees. "So shall thy seed be", as the light of the world.

Praying amiss is praying in ignorance of God's will; not having the knowledge of His will. Praying without an understanding of the mind of God concerning a situation will result in an ineffective solution, or not receiving any solution at all. Praying with an expectation, but without an inner vision will also result in keeping you unnecessarily long in expectation without any effective solution. The Disciples of Christ were praying with expectations and not with a vision when Peter was thrown into the prison. They were still expecting the release of Peter even when Peter had been released by the angel. They saw Peter as an angel (Acts 12:13-15).

Often, we consistently ask for the same thing, even when our demands have been released. The man at the beautiful gate was expecting to receive arms, when divine expectation with a perfect health to be able to walk and do things for himself was his actual area of need. God's divine expectation was not for him to remain a beggar, but to rise up from a beggarly attitude and be active. Does your expectation intertwine with His divine vision? One can pray his own will, confess his word, but not actually pray "according to God's will." "This is the confidence we have in God, when we pray according to his will; he heareth us" (1 John 5:14). Therefore, we are not just praying in multitude of words, being ignorant of the Father's will. The direction of God's thought in a situation makes the prayer effective and the consistency of your faith in this thought makes it fervent. "The effectual and fervent prayer of the righteous avails much" (James 5:6). "So shall thy seed be": as the light that shines brighter and brighter in all your situations.

RELATIONSHIP AND FELLOWSHIP

God's blessings are not based on relationship alone, but also on fellowship. Fellowship helps in renewing the mind, and positions your faith to receive God's blessings. It wards away fleshly lusts and desires that interfere with receiving his promises and living in fullness. It puts away unforgiveness, offences, fear, evil imaginations, and every other incessant manifestation of the flesh as stated in Gal. 5:19.

Your fellowship with God strengthens your fellowship with others and creates enough room for obedience. Above all, fellowship attracts God's presence that brings in joy and satisfaction in you. "Without faith it is impossible to please God; whosoever cometh to Him must believe that He is, and is a rewarder of them that diligently seek him" (Heb. 11:6). The key word in this passage is diligence. God measures and approves diligence in seeking him. Therefore, we must be persistent, in spite of all odds, discontentment, disappointments, and discouragements. Our love for Him should remain unshakable. This can only be accomplished through His strength that is acquired in fellowship with the Holy Spirit. "With Him, all things are possible to them that believe" (Matt 19:26). Fellowship with him makes all things possible, because it promotes your belief system, bringing us in agreement with His thoughts, and strengthens our faith to do the impossible.

The Holy Spirit is the energy of God. Through Him, God reads the mind of the believer. The Holy Spirit is our intercessor (Rom. 8:27). Our fellowship with the Holy Spirit constantly releases the thoughts of our hearts, corrects, aligns, and blends our thoughts with His thoughts. Next, the Holy Spirit transmits these thoughts to the Father. Fellowship with the Holy Spirit is the transforming light that lightens and glitters our thoughts to Him. "Likewise the Spirit also helpeth our infirmities, for we know not what to pray as we ought, but the Spirit itself maketh intercession for us with groaning that cannot be uttered. And he that searcheth the hearts knoweth what is the mind of the Spirit, because he maketh intercessions for the saints according to the will of God". (Rom 8: 26-27).

Our relationship with God positions us to fellowship with expectations. Our relationship entitles us to acquire benefits in Christ, but does not position us to receive them. Abraham's fellowship instilled obedience and direction that opened doors for God's promise for the coming Messiah. He did not only have a relationship with Him, but also his relationship with God opened his eyes to see and believe His promises. Therefore, his relationship brought him to a position of friendship with God; God completely and totally relied on his faithfulness as a friend. This could have only been accomplished in fellowship (Gen. 18:17-19). Abraham's communion with God gave him courage to leave his father's kindred and move to a land that God would show him (Gen. 12:1). His fellowship strengthened his faith that instilled his great obedience to this call. Furthermore, his friendship strengthened his faith to offer his only son, Isaac.

At a stage in his relationship with His twelve disciples, Jesus promoted them from the status of being servants to friends. He even expounded to them the positions, status and services of servants and friend. (Luke 17:7-10, Jn. 15:13-15). Friendship is not developed in one day; it could take some time to consider someone a friend. Solidifying friendship takes commitment and trust, which is satisfied in fellowship and communion. Even in our relationship with people around us. Many times we call people who are not really friends, our friends. Many people have faced a lot of disappointments, harassments, heartaches when betrayed. Jesus mark of true friendship is in the ability to discern what the will of God is, and to do it. Even Judas that betrayed him was tagged a friend, though he yielded himself to become used as instrument of betrayal.

More often than not, we feel so disappointed when betrayed by friends. We hate and take it on them not realizing that God's election is by Grace and such have been elected to carry out a mission. The Jews could not lay their hands on Jesus for the fear of the multitude. God allowed Satan to enter Judas for a divinely elected commission. So, quit living in bitterness and unforgiveness, because of God's ordained principle and line of action for your promotions through betrayals from your dear friends. Jesus did not tag his disciples friends the first time He met them. Friendship with them took a period of commitment and trust before He satisfactorily identified their friendship with revelation.

A defined relationship directs a defined commitment and service. Relationship must be accomplished with a defined purpose. This is being achieved though fellowship. When purpose is known, abuse and conflicts can be averted. "But as many as received Him, He gives power to become sons of God, even to them that believe on his name" (John 1:12). Therefore, the fruit or power of son-ship is realized in fellowship. Receiving and believing are both important in receiving the power of son-ship. The power of son-ship is seen in both the entitlement and the position to benefit from acquisition. Studying the word of God continuously in prayer controls our belief and strengthens our fellowship with God.

Look at the parable of the midnight friend: 'I say unto you, though he will not rise and give him because he is his friend, yet because of his importunity, he will rise and give him as many as he needed" (Luke 11:5-8). In this parable, Christ simply emphasized the truth that receiving from the Lord is not just based on relationship, but on intimacy and understanding. The friend understood his friend and did not give up in his demands. If he did not have adequate knowledge of who his friend was, he would have quit requesting. His persistence, irrespective of the negative response from his friend, gave him what he desired. How did he gain understanding of his friend? Understanding anyone can be realized through fellowship and interaction. He gained this understanding through fellowship. Fellowship builds a strong wall of commitment and trust in the parties concerned.

CHAPTER 9

The Seed as Abraham's Reward

God was Abraham's reward and still his reward from generation to generation. The only time we have the abundance we expect is when we make him our reward and not expect him to give us a reward only. We need His reward by receiving Him first to be the reward. Just like Abraham, our act of faith should make the person of God our satisfaction and the reward. This act of faith can only be produced and controlled by fellowship and communion. The Holy Spirit will then direct us to the act of faith that pleases him. Faith is not just affirmation of his word, but also faith is controlled by his virtues of love. For every act of faith, God is looking out for His virtue which includes peace, love, patience, longsuffering, humility, meekness, and temperance (Gal. 5:22; 2 Pet. 1:4-8). Growing and abounding in grace in all these virtues open great doors to His precious promises and keep our souls healthy in Him.

His strength is sufficient and helps us to abound in this grace. We are saved by grace. Salvation is a continuous process that requires continuous fellowship in Him, not losing focus of our calling. "Work out your salvation with fear and trembling" (Phil. 2:12); "But the salvation of the righteous is of the Lord, He is their strength in time of trouble, the Lord shall help them, and deliver them from the hand of the wicked because they trust in him"(Ps 37:39). Our deliverance is seen in the work of salvation which is purely seen in our act of faith and trust in his divine love. This trust is seen and manifested in the virtues of God.

God's promise to Abraham was released, when he saw his selfless act to the king of Sodom and to Melchizedek (Exod. 14:17-24). The Syrophonician daughter received her healing through the mother's act of humility. The woman with the issue of blood pressed her way through the crowd, not minding being trampled upon by the crowd. Even Rahab in the Old Testament despised the threats that would come from the Jericho king and saved the spies. Moses saw the riches in Egypt, yet he boldly refused to identify himself with Egypt, because he knew his identity

We must quit thinking that a relationship positions us to acquire blessings. Instead, we must reframe our minds to please the Lord by our act of faith, which is monitored by the Holy Spirit inside of us. Our act of faith and trust is seen in our works not just in our confession. Abraham did not confess faith, but acted in faith. This act of faith drew God's attention to be his reward first, before He rewarded Abraham with wealth or other possessions. This reward is still an ongoing reward in the nation of Israel till date. Every nation that recognizes and blesses the nation of Israel is still and remains a recipient of this reward, which was instilled by the faith of Abraham. Our act of faith attracts God's eternal reward seen and being manifested from generation to generation.

Abraham was and is still the father of nations. Fatherhood is not just physical and fleshly responsibility, but also an eternal responsibility that passes from age to age, from generation to generation. His act of faith gave him an eternal reward. "Children are the crown of old age, and the glory of the children are their fathers" (Prov. 17:6). "So shall thy seed be," an everlasting reward through your faith. "Against hope, believed in hope, that he might be the father of many nations, according to that which has been spoken" (Rom. 4:18). "So shall thy seed be," "The father of us all" (Rom. 4:16). An eternal responsibility passed on from generation to generation. You can also be a father or mother of many nations by the same kind of faith exhibited by Abraham, through the Seed inside of you.

CHAPTER 10

Seed As Our Eternal Reward

When we spend time to make God our reward through our act of fellowship, then He will reward accordingly. He becomes our eternal reward that does not only transform our lives but also the lives of our children, both born and unborn. He is eternity, and his reward extends far beyond your imaginations, just like the vast stars over the heavens. Remember, He gives exceedingly abundantly above that which we ask or imagine according to the power that works in us (Eph. 3:20). God gives according to the prosperity of our souls (John 3:1). To what power is he referring? He is referring to the power of faith and love of God living inside of us. The act of faith is selfless. Therefore, the act of faith is the exhibition of the nature of God, which is love. God does not have love; God is love. Therefore, when we act in love, we act in God, and acting in God releases God as the reward of our faith.

"Faith is the substance of things hoped for..." (Heb. 11:1). Substance means something tangible, something with which to hold, while waiting for the physical manifestation. We can move mountains, as we become prayer warriors. Our faith brings transformation when our minds are also renewed to the selfless nature of God. Then, we are ready to give all for the sake of Christ. Furthermore, we are ready to give sacrificially to the kingdom priests and kings, who are the children of God. Mechilzedech was a high priest in the order of Christ. We should be able to recognize the form of God in this life.

Many have missed their "reward," "God", because of insensitivity and inability to discern when God is passing their way. Yet, they kept confessing the word without understanding the direction to act. Act of faith precedes possession. Note that faith is the substance of things for which we "hoped." The word is "hoped" not "hope." This word is past tense, not present future or future tense. It is not the substance of what you are hoping to get but what you have already hoped to get. Therefore, your act of faith is not just confessing the word until you get what you wish. The act shows you have already received what you hoped for. When was the hope instigated? The very day you made the Lord your "Reward" at the revelation of Christ, the seed inside of you. You accepted Him with this hope. Thus, this is a past event. You are not, therefore, expecting to receive what He is about to give. Instead, you have already received His promises in Christ, which are "Yea and Amen."

This works with God's promises to Abraham of being his reward at the revelation of the seed. God told Abraham, "I am your reward." He did not say 'I am going to be your reward'. 'Against hope, Abraham believed in hope'. He believed in what he hoped for at the revelation of the seed, and this hope manifested Isaac through his obedience and faithfulness to God. Your fellowship with Him continuously manifests the hope, because it positions you to hear Him speak and obey Him. The substance of our hope is the virtue of God. God wants to see an aspect of His virtue in our faith, not just the confession. Your confession of faith is an aspect of the substance of the things for which you hoped. There is nothing new that God has not already accomplished. The old passed away, giving space for the new at the time you surrendered completely to his Lordship. The assignment on you was completed even before you knew it.

RECOGNIZING THE FORM OF GOD

The reality of God's word in our lives is in the ability to recognize the form of God. The promise to Abraham was in Christ. He recognized God in the form of Mechizedeck who came in the order of Christ. Mechizedeck was "...made like unto the Son of God" (Heb. 7:3). "The promises of God in Christ are yea and amen." We should, therefore, seek the order of Christ where God's promises are seated. These promises are seated in our priestly responsibility, where God expects sacrificial giving with selfless motives. What can we offer in order of Christ at all times? This could be our commitment to prayer, winning souls, exhorting one another, giving to the needs of the saints, forgiving and forbearing one another, and performing a great number of faith-activated works, and doing all in the love of God. Our act of faith is not limited to giving tithes and offerings in the congregation. Our giving must be backed up with love and not necessarily on what we can get. If God does not meet our expectation in giving us our desires, will we still be persistent in well doing? After all the giving at the church services, how do we spend the rest of our lives during the week?

We are saved by grace unto good works (Eph. 2:1-2). Good deeds do not justify us, but our justification is the entrance to good deeds. "Let your light so shine before men that they may see your good works and glorify your father who is in heaven" (Matt. 5:16). This means that God is glorified by good works of faith, not just good confessions of faith. Abraham offered a tenth of his spoil. Good works of faith are the symbols and epitome of faith. "Show me your faith, without works, and I will show thee my faith by my works" (James 2:15-18). Faith without works is like a body without a Spirit. That is to say, it is dead. Abraham at Mamre recognized the form of God and called the three men Lord (Gen. 18:1). He was ready to give all to make a dwelling place for God and to bring to birth God's promise.

God can come to you in form of a child. Furthermore, he can come in form of a stranger. He can even come in the form of the poor and the oppressed, a brother or a sister in need, your kids, an unsaved soul that needs Jesus, or a brother or sister who offends you. How can you see the dirt on the feet of someone else if those feet do not step on you? Offences coming from people are not to weigh you down. Instead, they are opportunities to see dirt and wash off the dirt through prayers and supplications, and practical helps. Jesus admonishes us to wash one another's feet even as He did. You are indebted to wash your spouse's feet, your father's feet, or anyone who has offended you. "If I then, your Lord and Master, have washed your feet, ye also ought to wash one another's feet" (John 13:14).

You are expected to show kindness even to your enemies. Although it may seem impossible to do this, your fellowship with God makes it easier. Remember, "With Him, all things are possible." Act of faith requires total dependence on Him. Faith requires absolute confidence in God to demonstrate love even when it looks and seems impossible to love. Faith is not just an act to believe that God will provide material acquisitions, but faith also depends on God's strength to walk in love. "Greater love has no man than this, that a man should lay down his life for his friends" (John 16:13). What is love? Love is an act of faith that allows us to accomplish things that would otherwise be impossible, just to please God. The good works are pleasing to God, because they are done in faith. Faith is the attitude and corresponding actions that demonstrate what we believe. It is the act of obedience towards God's word. All the faith giants in Hebrew 11, demonstrated faith through their attitudes and/or actions. It is the substance of things hoped for (Heb 11:1). Substance means tangibility

Offences are stepping-stones to victories, because they create an opportunity to grow and serve the Lord in love and unity. They give you opportunity to pray and trust God well enough for someone's victory to love God and eliminate self-gratification and vainglory. Separation from people might lead you to forget them, but not necessarily forgiving them. However, not forgiving them, or unforgiveness itself, is an entrance to bondage, guilt, and shame from which the Lord has set us free.

God could come in the form of a "certain man" who needs one form of help. Our faith in Christ directs us to good works in Him. "Who gave himself for us that He might redeem us from iniquity, and purify unto himself a peculiar people, zealous of good works" (Titus 2:14). Remember that the invisible things of God from the creation of the world are clearly seen by the things that are made. He is the invisible made visible by the things we see (Rom. 1:20). The invisible is made visible by the abundance of the stars. Furthermore, the invisible is made visible in the order of Christ. The order of Christ is like the stars of heaven. They are innumerable, yet in order. So, are a countless number of people are set across our way to affect positively. We are a kingdom of priests and kings" (Rev. 5:10) in God's domain.

Then shall the righteous answer him saying, "Lord, when saw we thee, hungered, and we fed thee? Or thirsty and gave thee drink . . . and the King shall answer and say unto them, verily I say unto you, inasmuch as you did it to the least of these my brethren, you have done it unto me" (John 25:35-40). Your eternity is defined by God's love residing in you. It is not determined by how much acquisition is kept to oneself, but how much distribution of sacrificial love of visitations made in time of needs. It is not assessed by how anointed or gifted you are. Instead, your eternity is assessed by how much of the anointing and gifts have been utilized to change lives and situations. "So shall thy seed be" - a life changer. "A man's life does not consist on the abundance of things possessed" (Luke 12:15). Instead, I believe that life consists of the abundance of things distributed in love.

CHAPTER 11

Sowing of the Seed

The seed is sown as eternal seed. Whatever you give or sow attracts eternal reward. God sowed for eternal reward; therefore, that which you have sown today is in everlasting remembrance. "The righteous shall be in everlasting remembrance" (Ps. 112:6). "He hath dispersed abroad. He hath given to the poor: His righteousness remaineth forever" (2 Cor. 9:10). "So shall thy seed be." The seed you sow is not just for a temporary harvest, but the seed yields a permanent and eternal harvest. Thus, our harvest time is eternal. Giving to the need of saints is not just a temporary investment, but also an eternal investment that attracts eternal reward. "So shall thy seed be." Your seed will be remembered and that justifies your faith and establishes your righteousness from generation to generation.

"God is not unrighteous to forget your work and labor of love in that you have ministered to the saints and yet minister" (Heb. 6:10). "He that reapeth receiveth wages and gathereth fruit unto life eternal that both he that soweth and he that reapeth may rejoice together. And herein is that saying true, one soweth and another reapeth. I sent you to reap whereon you bestowed no labor, other men labored and ye are entered into their labor" (John 4:36-38).

The generations to come are recipients of your labor of sowing. We are also recipients of generational blessings that proceed from the good works of faith of our parental genealogy. Remember, He is a God of generations. He is God of Abraham, Isaac, and Jacob. You reap from where you did not labor to sow. "Remembering without ceasing your work of faith and labor of love, and patience of hope in our Lord Jesus

Christ in the sight of God and our Father. . . . So that ye are examples to all that believe in Macedonia and Achaia . . .but also in every place your faith to God-ward spread abroad so that we need not to speak anything" (1 Thess. 1:3-9). "That He would grant you according to the riches of His glory, to be strengthened with might by His Spirit in the inner man" (Eph. 3:16). "Now unto Him that is able to do exceedingly abundantly above all that we ask or think, according to the power that worketh in us" (Eph. 3:20).

We often think that the power being referred to here is just the power to believe and receive what we need. We need to bear in mind that faith is the substance of a past event, of "things hoped for" and not things for which we are hoping. He is not referring to the power that we are hoping to receive but power that we had already received. That power is consistent in well doing. Furthermore, that power never gives up, because He had already tasted the victory. The level of commitment of this power inside of us determines the level of results to be obtained. He is referring to the ability to remain encouraged and be constant in well doing amidst all discouragements and hopelessness. Substance is something tangible. So the measure of our faith depends on the measure with which this power in us is working to keep us at peace and rejoicing in that which we already had hoped on.

Faith, therefore, is not complete without a defined hope. Believing to receive what is yet to come is not faith, but a work motivated by the belief that we had already received is faith. "When you pray, believe that you have received and ye shall have whatsoever you ask" (Math 11: 23). This means that your faith is not necessarily hoping to receive, but a hope that you had already received., and your actions will be controlled by such hope. Remember, faith is the 'substance' of things hoped for Heb 11:1 not the 'substance' of things you are hoping for. Substance is something tangible

POWER IN WAITING

We persistently work for our employers, expecting to get our wages at a certain time in the month. The very day you were employed, you already hoped to receive your wages at an agreed time; your hope was established the very day you received the employment letter. Our employers are recipients of our good work of faith. Even when we do not feel like being at work, we still have to get there any way. A certain element of power motivates us to work. Perhaps the wages we expect to receive in spite of all odds is a motivator. Thus, we are like being motivated to complete difficult tasks for the things hoped. There is no doubt in your mind that you will receive the wages, because it was established when you received your employment letter.

The same concept goes when we pray. At the time of prayer, an agreement has already gone forth with you and the Father that you have already received your heart desire and that is the day the hope is established. This is the time you received the employment letter of assurance. You are not hoping to receive, but looking forward to the manifestation. Glory!

What power is He then referring to in this context that must work in us? This is the power of being persistent in our well doing. This is the power to remain in obedience of love and giving to the needs of saints and unbelievers even when our flesh is not willing. Even when we feel discouraged, that motivational power must still work inside of us. How do we gain access to that power?

We can gain such power by consistently remaining in prayer and asking for strength instead of reminding Him every day of His promises to receive what we want or desire. We should spend more time in His word and request the power to remain in faith with expectations. The power eliminates our doubt in God's promises. The resurrection power of His presence allows us to act and demonstrate faith. With this power working and being revealed from the inside of us, we will be sure of the manifestation of the things hoped.

"We know that we have passed from death to life, because we love the brethren. He that loveth not his brother abideth in death . . . and ye know that no murderer hath eternal life in him. Hereby perceive we the love of God, because he laid down his life for us, we ought to lay down our lives for the brethren. But whosoever hath this world's good, and seeth his brother have need, and shutteth up his bowel of compassion from him, how dwelleth the love of God in him?" (1 John 3:14-17). Therefore, the inability to distribute is a lack of eternity. God has the power to demonstrate love as we wait on Him. If you need healing, ask for power to pray and minister to the sick.

If you need marriage restoration, request for power to restore someone else's ailing marriage. "And let us not be weary in well doing for in due season we shall reap if we faint not" (Gal. 6:9). The words are "due season." The employer and employee already agree on the time and terms of payment of wages. This is not the case with our heavenly Father. Instead, God alone determines the time and terms of payment. Your responsibility is strictly to be obedient and remain strong in His might of well doing.

We are of the seed of Abraham; therefore, his spirit rests in us. Abraham is the father of us all, through his eternal spirit. He remained steadfast in his love for God. He did not faint nor did he grow weary until Isaac came. He did not stagger at the promises of God, and even at the offering of Isaac, he still believed God. He was not discouraged. Abraham's righteousness endures forever. It is eternal, because of his exceeding faith. It is an eternal recommendation of faith by God. He remained in the power of faith to please God at his waiting, rather than in the power to keep confessing. He did not stagger in his acts of faith, and he did not stagger in his confessions of faith. This righteousness possessed by faith endures in us because we are of the seed of Abraham. It is an everlasting righteousness.

Faith is the substance of things hoped for. The word again is 'substance' which means tangibility. We should move further from just confessing his word to acting on his word. This puts more meaning to our faith. The kingdom of God is not in words but in the demonstration of his power" (1 Cor 4:20). What power? The power to love God; the power to apply his wisdom and direction to fulfill destiny.

Jesus prayed for Peter to remain in faith even when he saw the Devil's intending strategies to seize him. He did not ask the Lord to eliminate the oncoming onslaught against Peter's faith, but requested empowerment to stay in faith, so that he could be instrumental in the uplifting of his brethren's faith. Jesus knew the consequences that could visit Peter if he became weary in faith. Therefore, standing firm and not becoming discouraged was essential in accomplishing his task in the ministry, which was to receive the crown of his reward. The power to remain in faith and love for him is most essential, and this was the overcoming power. "This is the victory that overcomes even our faith" (1 John 5:4).

CHAPTER 12

A Covenant Seed

The generational package of blessings from this seed shall be eternal. "He that believed in him shall not perish but have an everlasting life" (John 3:16). Our lives in Christ are eternal. Like the stars of heaven that can never perish, our lives will linger from generation to generation. His righteousness shall be forever and his salvation from generation to generation. (Isa. 51:8). The Seed is therefore, the fulfillment of an eternal covenant with man. Thus, the Seed of God in me and in you can never be eroded. The blessing from this Seed is passed on from generation to generation. The generational children are partakers of the blessings that flow from this Seed. The covenant with him is eternal, because it lingers from generation to generation. It is an everlasting covenant (Gen. 17: 13). The righteous shall be in everlasting remembrance. "The righteous is an everlasting foundation. The memory of the righteous is blessed" (Prov. 10: 7, 25).

I have often heard parents tell their kids that they have the responsibility of making choices in their lives. I partially disagree with this concept. The destiny of a child is partly determined by the choice made by the parents. A right choice of delighting in the Lord and fearing him creates room for generational choices (Ps. 112:1-2, 128:1-3). The right choices made by parents give these children proper directions in making their own choices and bettering their lives. God gives preference to men or women to make their own choices, but God's utmost expectation is for mankind to choose to serve him; God expects this choice to be under parental guidance. God expects parents to produce children who are likeminded in Christ.

Have you lost all hopes on getting your child back on track? Are you weary of speaking to ears that do not seem to comprehend? Have you given up hope on your run away child? Listen to the voice of the Lord. Your choice in Christ has made or will make the difference. Your covenant lineage in Christ affects your child, even the unborn. God is in the hopeless situation, because of your covenant lineage in Christ Jesus the Seed. "For the unbelieving husband is sanctified . . . else were your children unclean, but now are they holy" (1 Cor. 7, 14). A child does not make the decision of being holy. Holiness is imputed on him through holiness in one or both parents.

Instilling God's character in these kids will make them mighty. We teach by examples. The lives we live in their presence are much more transferable than what we say. Even when it looks like they are not living the transferred lives, remember that the Seed can never be aborted. The seed is already planted in them and shall be like the stars of heaven. It is an everlasting seed that transforms lives in due season. Every planting in their lives through your work of faith is eternal and remains eternal in the heart of him that has called you to his honor and grace. There is no disappointment in eternity. "So shall thy seed be." "Out of the abundance of the heart, the mouth speakest" (Matt. 12:34). The rod of discipline, or corrections comes out of the abundance of love in Christ Jesus (thy seed) to and properly align their decision making with God's plan for their lives.

POWER OF THE TONGUE

The words we speak are seeds that live or die. "Death and life are in the power of the tongue and a man's belly is satisfied with the fruit of his mouth, and with the increase of his lips shall he be filled" (Prov. 18:20-21). The Bible says "in the power of the tongue" not "in the tongue."

The power of the tongue comes from the power of love in the heart, and this determines the measure of impact we make on the kids and in our mentorship. Do not correct or discipline a child with anger, because you are transferring the spirit of aggression into the child. When we start visualizing the negative behavior and unwholesome attitudes as they affect God, rather than the way they affect us, this will build up passion within us and position us to correct with love than correcting with anger. Their choices are fully dependent on transference of spirit. Such transfers will likely direct their choices.

God blessed them and said, "Be fruitful and multiply" (Gen. 1:28). To be fruitful and multiply means to procreate and to prosper in spirit, soul, and body. It is possible for one to have twelve children, yet unproductive. One is unproductive when these kids live without Christ, evidently seen in their foolish and faithless acts in the society. Productivity and multiplication are the kingdom's assets that are only found in Christ Jesus. Even though the covenant seed was passed on to the Jews, today, we are recipients of this covenant promise. **Success is how much that have been transferred to posterity, and not just how much have been achieved.** God placed us on a better covenant so that He might fulfill his promise to Abraham. Christ in us is the hope of God's glory. The hope of the Abraham covenant was passed on to the church and the Jews. God passed on the hope of destiny! "So shall thy seed be" a covenant seed!

SOUL WINNING

Fruitfulness and multiplication are also seen in evangelism, simply defined as the winning of souls into the kingdom of God. Furthermore, fruitfulness is also an eternal investment for every believer. It is an opportunity that supersedes every business opportunity. This opportunity resides in the power of the tongue. It is an opportunity that awaits every child of God; however, it is a mandatory opportunity.

What makes fruitfulness an eternal investment? Simply stated in Dan 12:3, "And they that are wise shine as the brightness of the firmament and they that turn many to righteousness as the stars for ever and ever". "He that winneth souls is wise" (Prov. 11:30). Wisdom is seen in soul winning and turning souls to God. The Bible describes the reward as being as the "stars forever and ever." This means that soul winning is also an eternal recommendation with an eternal reward. God commends highly anyone involved in this as an investor with eternal and generational blessings. Such a person will continuously shine from generation to generation, thereby becoming an extension of the covenant Seed. This is mandatory for every Christ's blood covenant bought believer.

CHAPTER 13

The Anointing of the Seed

The seed is God's word that carries the anointing. What is the anointing and the purpose of the anointing? When purpose is not known, abuse becomes inevitable. Anointing is God's power on earth that is manifest through his word (seed) that is inside of us.

The oil is just the material through which it flows and not the anointing itself. When the word of God penetrates and saturates the oil, it ceases to be ordinary oil, and becomes supernatural oil called anointing oil. Whenever God directs the use of the anointing oil, both in the new and old testaments, a message always goes with it. The Lord directed Moses on the preparation of the anointing oil and specifically stated its use: "Thou shall make it an oil of holy ointment, an ointment compound after the art of apothecary; it shall be a holy anointing oil" (Exod. 30:25). "And thou shalt sanctify them, that they may be holy: whatsoever toucheth them shall be holy" (Exod. 30:29). The purpose of the anointing is to keep holy anyone who touches, or comes in touch with the oil.

God instructed Elijah to anoint Elisha in his stead. Hazeal was to be the king of Syria, and Jehu was to be the king of Israel. Samuel was sent to anoint Saul as the king of Israel, and David was anointed for the throne. These anointing was for the authority of kingship. Elisha sent Gehazi his servant to touch the dead son of the Shunamite woman with Elisha's staff. The child did not wake up until Elisha laid on him and put a breath in his nostrils. The anointing was on Elisha, and not on Gehazi. Though Gehazi had the staff, Elisha carried the anointing within (1King4:31-35). We have often used the anointing oil without an adequate knowledge of its use, and, therefore, we might think that it is ineffective. "Where there is no vision, the people perish" (Prov. 29:18).

We now need to take a critical look at the anointing of the Holy Spirit and the message of the anointing. The star stays permanently in its position from year to year and never loses its power. Even the three wise men followed the direction of the stars to meet with the holy child Jesus at the manger. The star was sent on an errand, and every star has a specific identity of glory and message from the Lord (1 Cor. 15:41). "The morning stars sang together, and all the sons of God shouted for joy" (Job 38:7). The stars are sent to sing for the joy of the sons of God. "So shall thy seed be."

THE MISSION OF THE ANOINTING

In the same way, and at any point in time, the anointing of the seed carries with him a message I could call "the message of the anointing". Each time we ask for an increase in anointing, God expects us to know the need for the anointing. There is always a specific assignment for the specific anointing resting on you. It is, therefore, insignificant when you request for an anointing without requesting for the purpose of the anointing. The Holy Spirit is the anointing. Anointing comes with a responsibility, and every vessel of God has special anointing that is deposited on him.

"The Spirit of the Lord is upon me for he has anointed me to preach the gospel to the poor [and] heal the broken hearted . . . ." (Luke 4: 18,19). The anointing on Jesus was specific regarding his ministry. Jesus identified the mission of the anointing. Our daily submission to the Sprit of God releases the mission of the anointing. As we submit to one another in fear and reverence to the Lord, we submit to a specific power or anointing that works in that vessel. Submission is from the heart and the power to receive the anointing is in the power of submission. Some people have fellowshipped with a congregation of believers for years, yet they have experienced no change in their lives. Two things could be responsible:

1. Inability to discern if the message of the anointing on the leadership is what God really desires for us.
2. If our positioning is not in accordance with our divine placement, we might not be willing to submit, to listen, and to be obedient to the anointing. The heart could become proud.

Therefore, please take time to ask God if you are really in the right place of fellowship. Of all the prophets in Israel, Elijah was sent to the Zerapheth woman, because the anointing on Elijah carries the message for the Zerapheth. The Zerapheth received her miracle, because she submitted to the message of anointing. Many Christians have stood long waiting for a breakthrough because of insensitivity, lack of vision, and lack of direction to the anointing that carries their messages. The Lord puts us in the body as it pleases him, not as it pleases us. Let us quit attending church services just because the preacher preaches good messages, but ask God if the anointing carries the messages specifically meant for us.

For every message of the anointing, the purpose is to transform your life. The anointing is never ineffective. The main reasons stated above could be the reason of unfruitfulness in one's life, or when he or she is in the right place at the wrong time. The anointing might even be passing everyday in front of one's house just like the Shunamite woman, but one might not identify him or her because of spiritual blindness. Of all the multitude of impotent folks, the anointing singled out the man at the pool of Bethsaida. The anointing can also single you out if he carries your message. The anointing with your message might even be in the same work area with you. The anointing meant for our breakthrough may or may not even be the preaching from the pulpit. Ask the Lord to direct you to the anointing. The son of the Shunnamite woman did not experience the power of God to rise up from death, because the message of anointing was upon Elisha and not Gehazi, even though Gehazi held Elisha's mantle.

You must remember that you carry God's anointing upon your life, and God places many ministerial gifts in the body for uniformity. Submitting to one another's gift in the body will produce strong and dynamic powers that will greatly explode in these last days. The message of anointing is permanent and eternal. It is not temporal. You might quit running from one congregation to the other or from one relationship to the other just because you want a self-fulfillment. When God positions you and places that message on you, the message remains there. Even when you relocate, the anointing remains.

In Ps. 89:37, the holy oil anointed on David was to fight the battle for David, strengthen God's faithfulness and mercy, and promote His glory. Of all the prophets in Israel, Samuel anointed David, but Samuel did not remain with David. Nevertheless, this anointing protected David against the onslaughts of Saul. David took these messages back to God (in verse 3), when these messages were not being fulfilled. He understood God's messages at his anointing, and when this was not being fulfilled, he went back to God to inquire in verse 48-52. God cannot promise through the messages in the anointing without fulfillment of these messages. Anytime anointing oil comes on you with spoken words, take time to write these words down, because you will remind God of these words in your situations, just like David did.

Anointing can come with a pressing and squeezing. The olive oil has to be separated from the source. Then the oil must be pressed, crushed, and squeezed to extract the oil from the tissues before it can be used.

Thus, the oil takes on a transformation before it can be used. In the same way, we go through a transformation: We are squeezed, pressed, and crushed before we can be used. We have to go through a process, just like the olive fruit. We also need to be separated from the flesh for effective usage. Jesus also was crushed before His exaltation. He learned obedience through His suffering; therefore, He is our perfect example (1 Pet. 2:21). The harder the processing, the heavier the anointing will be. The anointing carries the message of your processing journey. Do not faint or grow weary in crushing situations, because these situations are for the increase of anointing in the vessel. The vessel is separated for the master's use. This anointing, remember is being prepared for a specific message. It is called the anointing of the seed.

CHAPTER 14

The Seed is in Control

The seed does not control choices, but is in control of the choices. God demands that we make the right decisions for our own good. He does not enforce any decisions or choices on humanity. Instead, He prefers and allows our willingness to make decisions. However, He wishes us to root our decisions in his word. God did not create us to be robots to be controlled and ruled against our own decisions. Consequently, the Lord expects us to treat our kids the same way. He expects our kids to be able to have absolute trust in him in their decision-making. We are only exhorted to train and to direct them in the way that they should go. We are not expected to control choices they make but to be in control of the choices they make. The act of being in control of the choices they make can only be done, and is effective through our prayers, and counseling in love. Wrong choices can be eliminated. Trying to control or impose our choices on the kids provokes them to anger (Eph. 6:4).

This also applies to spiritual mentorship, either in counseling, in pasturing, or in teaching. Whatsoever we do, it should be according to the measure of faith given to us. Any attempt to step beyond the boundary tends toward manipulation and control, which is devilish. God has given us the freedom to make our own choices, and in the same way, we should give the kids and spiritual children freedom to make their own choices and decisions in life. Tell them what is best for them, and let them make their choices. The fire of the Lord consumed the burnt sacrifice, wood, stones, and dust. The fire even licked up the waters from the trench on Mount Carmel and created room to make a right decision (1 Kings 18:38). The fire of decision should burn from the inside enabling a powerful tool for decision-making. Let our tools for decision-making be in our prayers, so that the decisions will be linked through his word. The word of the Lord is fire. This fire is like a two-edged sword that can cut asunder and consume wrong decisions.

Just like Elijah, we can only be in control through prayers and obedience. Our daily submission to God's divine principles, wisdom, and acts of discipline instills the fear of God in our children. Therefore, our actions are much more effective than our constant repetition of words. If our kids only hear what we say without seeing our actions, they start seeing us more as talkers than as trainers. As a result, our words alone become fleshly and intimidating, or manipulative, rather than stronger and sharper than a two-edged sword. "Having in readiness to revenge all disobedience, when your obedience is fulfilled" (2 COR 10:6).

PARENT- CHILD RELATIONSHIP

Many parents have lost the respect and obedience of their children, because they try to work things out themselves by controlling the children's decision-making, rather than being in control. Remember, the seed is in control not you and knows what is best for Him. Parents should pay more attention to challenges and emotions that may lead to depression, inordinate affections and so on. Insensitivity to the feelings allows the enemy to take advantage of it and direct children to outrageous negative solutions to their problems. We have a high priest that is touched by the feelings of our emotions and feelings of disappointments and has positioned us to do the same for others and our children, and take such feelings to the cross. How many times have we tried to reason out issues with our children rather than imposing our own ideologies on them thinking that they are God's instigated ideas? Do we take time to know where they are coming from with their own ideas first, reason these out with them through interactive discussions, especially with the days we are living in now with new technology innovations and millennial ways of seeing and analyzing issues? They are kingdom children and need kingdom approach to teachings and re-direction. Being in control requires more acts of persistent prayer, rather than acts of persistent repetitions of the same words. Seeking and receiving wisdom through prayers to redirect them accordingly instead of brushing aside their ideas and emotions will eliminate frustrations, discontentment and resentments, insubordination, depression to mention a few, but will rather give then proper direction of focus, confident and trust. Prayer is an act of love that proves that you are more concerned with a child's attitude or behavior as it affects God, than as it affects you. Such attitude in love for God releases power to destroy any act of disobedience or rebellion. "[You must have] a readiness to revenge all disobedience, when your obedience is fulfilled" (2 Cor. 10:6).

Directing a child with a right motive puts less emotional stress on parents, than directing them with a wrong motive. God expects us to put Him first in all corrections and disciplines we enforce on them. Prayers redirect your children's focus and allow them a better chance to right decisions. God's word is true. The words that issue from your prayers are incorruptible. The seed of the righteous is in everlasting remembrance. God's timing and move will surely redirect the child's choice and decisions. The seed inside of you is remembered forever. Every word of correction and rebuke inspired by love and not by anger is always in total submission and authority of the living God. These words must be remembered and applied in their lives at the fullness of time. Incorruptible seed can never be aborted. This is why no child of God should ever give up at a child's rebellious stage in life. No child of yours can be left behind. "So shall thy seed be." Incorruptible seed that will yield quality fruit in time in their lives at maturity.

Love of God covers a multitude of sins. Covering your children in prayers releases abundant mercies on them, waiting for God's infinite wisdom to excel in their lives with time. As parents, submitting to God's word is showing an act of obedience that can redirect and refocus our children's attention. We should know that whatever we do, even in secret, will surely reflect on the lives of the children. We cannot do anything on our own. However, if we depend and trust in the Lord daily to guide us in obedience, we will instill such acts of obedience in our children. Eli perished with the two children Hophni and Phinehas, not only because he did not restrain their contemptible sins, but because he did not cover them in prayers, asking for God's infinite mercies. Eli consented to God's decision to wipe out the entire household; "It is the Lord, Let him do what seems good to him" (1Sam3:18). I believe the mercy of the Lord would have overshadowed God's decision if Eli had pleaded for mercy.

"Be fruitful, multiply!" (Gen1:28). Multiplication is an act of productivity. Our obedience to God's word makes it easier for our children to honor our words too. Our obedience eliminates and burns out acts of rebellion from our children. God only avenges disobedience when our obedience is fulfilled (2Cor. 10:6). Remember, the first generation of Adam, Cain and Abel, were wiped out. Adam's rebellious spirit was released in Cain. Let us spend more time with God by trusting in his abundant grace and mercy to submit daily to his will and not to give in to our will. Even in trials and detestable situations, God wants to see our consistency in our faith by working with him.

A command for children to obey their parents was for kids being raised by Godly parents (Eph. 6:1). This is the only commandment with a promise of a long life span. This is because a parent in the Lord is in the love of God. It makes it a lot easier to understand that such a parent is positioned to give the child the right counsel from the Word. Not only giving the right counsel, noting also that any rebellious acts amongst the kids can easily be avenged through the parent's submission and loyalty to God. God's interest is not to ponder continuously on mistakes, but to turn every act of misleading directions into miracles, knowing that we are still putting on the coat of flesh. "Our weaknesses are made perfect in his strength" (2 Cor. 12:9). He does not depend on the ability of our children's strength to subdue. Instead, God depends on our own faith to eliminate every unlawful lifestyle.

CHAPTER 15

Honored Seed in Honored Marriage

Some outstanding truths will bring awesome changes in our marriage relationships. God's mystery in creation remains outstanding, when he blessed and declared fruitfulness in Adam. Amazingly, the woman was still inside the man when God "blessed them." God did not "bless him" only. Marriage is God's ordained covenant, ratified by the blood of Jesus (the Seed). This suggests that a godly soul mating breeds godly children. Any time the woman is no longer or is not in the man, there is a problem in that relationship. A Godly character among the children, which comes with increased faith and loyalty to God by the parent(s), will be lacking in that relationship. This problem consequently affects the children in their decision-making and life style.

Some children have taken to drugs, drinking, smoking, and participating in different kinds of incessant ungodly behavior, simply because of the disruption of marriage relationships. Statistically, more than 85% of present-day relationships are not built on solid marriage relationships. Many children from broken marriages grow up and decide to procreate without getting into a committed relationship, just because they are discouraged by the high rate of divorce in our society today. To them, marriage is more or less a risky transaction than a mutual commitment to one another. This has been a trend in recent years. The children have no role models at home.

Many children are being raised today by single parents. The original plan of God for procreation and productivity is being molested by human ideas and decrees. Even in our churches today, many single adults are involved in unhealthy relationships. The recent trends and common words we hear often are these: "I am living with my boyfriend, or I am living with my girlfriend." The covenant of marriage is no longer of great value to some people. It is high time the church woke up from her slumber against this ungodly trend. We must visualize the next move of God in this present era, resisting this strategic onslaught of the enemy on the church today.

THE SEED AND DIVORCE

I have seen marriages that waited on the Lord as long as 20-25 years for changes, peace, and restorations; yet, such marriages did not stand the test of time. The question one will therefore, ask is this: Is God who hates putting away in support of this divorce rate, or is the Devil responsible? With this increase in the divorce rate, what shall be the fate of our children, and what is God's plan for the born and unborn generations? What plan does God have to curb these unhealthy relationships that are breeding unhealthy fruits in the land? The preceding chapters of this book will be considering some possible solutions to these questions as the spirit helps us.

THE SEED: A SOLID FOUNDATION

The foundation and pillar of every house is what holds the house strong. If the foundation is not strong, the house could crumble with time. The pillar of the house must stand on a solid foundation. The pillar must have enough forces to withstand any severe weather conditions. The destructions of buildings by severe weather conditions, like hurricanes and tornadoes, is not only because the house is not on a solid ground, but also because the force of the severe thunderstorm is against the buildings. It can only take a greater force of opposition to resist the effects. If the house possesses such greater strength, then it becomes impossible to succumb to such traumatic devastations on the building. The Lord's arm is not short that he cannot save and deliver his own.

Only the relationship that is born of God can stand any test of shaking. Such are marriages that are built on solid foundations and held by strong pillars of love and faith in God. "Whatsoever is born of God overcomes the world; and the victory that overcomes is our faith" (1 John 5:4). The word here is "whatsoever" and not "whosoever." This means to me that any relationship that is not born of God will not overcome, no matter how long we have waited. The ones that withstand the storm of trials and shakings are the ones set up on God's solid foundation. These pillars are built by love and faith in God's arm of mercies. *Even if both parties married in unbelief,* God still makes ready for the intended future, as long as the relationship is born of God. After divorce, the relationship can still be healed. What is born of God is victorious and eternal because the seed is eternal.

What God does is permanent and must yield and remain fruitful through faith in Christ. Are you separated, divorced, or going through a divorce? Tornado warnings depict two things: heavy out pouring of rain and a warning to go to the safest corner for safety. The thickness of the clouds depicts an outpouring of rain that brings massive flooding. Therefore, the situation is either for your deliverance and safety and/or for an outpouring of God's blessings.

Every plant that God himself has not planted must be rooted out. No other foundation can be laid except that which God himself has laid. Therefore, if the foundation of any relationship is not grounded and rooted in God and there is no strong pillar to hold them together, it will never stand the test of time. However, couples can reverse the foundation, even if the foundation is on a generational curse, ignorance, fleshly lust and desires, or infatuations, the redemptive power of Christ can save the marriage.

CHAPTER 16

Soulmating in Marriage

God has been in the process and is still in the process of delivering souls. *Marriage is soul mating.* A kingdom that rises against each other cannot stand. God demands that we should be on the safest corner before receiving the rain of a Godly covenant relationship, which is built on a solid and Godly foundation.

That which is fleshly is fleshly. Some people go into a deep relationship while still in sin. In that relationship, one of the parties could encounter Christ. God still permits a continuity in that relationship, if the unbelieving spouse decides to stay in that relationship (1 Cor. 7:12-13). The reason is that the righteous seed in the believing spouse acts as a covering, but does not have control over his or her decision-making. The Lord allows the soul's communion, until the unbelieving decides to leave.

The question now is this: when truly does a man or woman leave or depart from a relationship? If marriage is soul mating, a departure or divorce creates a detachment of souls. Divorce, in the spiritual point of view, is not when you are served the divorce certificate from the courtroom, but truly takes place when one soul is detached from the other. The divorce certificate is a ruling by law that certifies what has been contracted. Many people have suffered painfully from a divorce, because they lacked discernment of the things happening around them, neither do they have understanding what the word God is saying in their condition. Some have lost their precious lives in an attempt to make the relationship work.

They have also passed through unrealistic pains, because they lacked understanding of God's strategic programs. They do not actually know or realize when their soul mate has actually detached. Two people can still live together, but they are strangers to each other and not actually husband and wife. One soul has already detached; making the two people live together just as strangers to each other. I am not in favor of divorce, but this is to create an awareness of God's divine grace to keep minds in perfect peace in the midst of marital turbulence.

MARITAL FOUNDATIONS

God is in the business of separating the tares from the wheat. He is in the business of doing a massive shaking, and every foundation that is shaken must be removed. God cannot pour a new wine in an old wineskin. Every tree that is not bringing forth fruit must be hewn down. He is longsuffering and does not desire any saved soul to be in perpetual, self inflicted pains. God's agenda is for the soul mates to enjoy their relationship. However, if the marriage is broken, God can still repair it. Separation does not necessarily mean divorce. The period of separation could be a period of hibernation and reassessment for the couples. Thereafter, the marriage is rebuilt, renewed, and sealed by his infinite power and grace.

This message will bring solace to the single, and divorced adults who are still hurting. We must stop holding on to an ungodly relationship that God wants us to let go. It does not matter how long you have been in the relationship. If God says let go, let go! "Whatsoever is born of God overcomes the world, and this is the victory that overcomes the world, even our faith" (1John 5:4). The word there is 'Whatsoever' and not 'Whosoever' and that includes marriages. So if any relationship is not born of God, it will not stand.

The relationship that is coming between you and your eternal destiny might no longer be a part of your story. Restoration comes from

Him for His unique purpose and opportunities. You are not your own, and what you think is detestable to you, could be God's avenue into your freedom in Christ Jesus. Stop holding what God wants you to let go. He is the God who can dethrone and enthrone kings. Only God can bring you to your expected end. Your story is in His hands. "So shall thy seed be", to set you free from an ungodly and unfruitful relationship. He can still rebuild broken walls and restore destroyed gates in the relationship. Only work toward his agenda and not yours. Just like the stars shine out of the thick clouds of darkness after a storm, God can lead you into the clear understanding of His agenda. All tragedies of life are for activating inbuilt ministries for generations to come. "So shall thy seed be"; as the stars of heaven.

I have come to realize that the way God moves his children still points toward eternity. Some broken relationships are for deliverance and restoration of souls. The shepherd is aware of where the sheep is (Ps. 23:1-2). God is more interested in delivering souls. The new birth episode is the first step to restoration of souls (Eph. 1:14). The power of God works from the inside, setting souls free from unhealthy relationships.

Some societies and even some believers see divorce as a taboo and most people, especially from the married circle withdraw contact, relationship and communication with the divorced. Christ came for the rejected ones. He did not come to blame, or condemn, but to seek the divorced also and comfort them. So, resenting the divorced does not exhibit the love nor does it transcend the mind of God in the church. To these set of people, I would rather advise that leaning solely on God's understanding can deliver them of this hateful act.

The Samaritan woman at the pool was accepted having mingled with different men. Jesus understood her predicament, and with kind words, He brought her out of the loneliness and seeking for acceptance which led her to sleeping with different men. She became an evangelist instantly at her deliverance (John 4:15-19,28-30). The church needs to arise and embrace the divorced and the widows with an understanding of God's revealed program of forgiveness, acceptance and love that exalts. This does not apply to marriage relationships only, but also to every relationship that is not on a solid foundation with a pillar of faith and love. You might find yourself lonely as if God has rejected you. No! It is all about His jealousy over our soul. He is the husband of the widow (Isa. 53:5). Widowhood here means "the lonely and the rejected."

Those things we cannot see, He sees. Those who do not appreciate our worth, He takes out of our green light, not only for the benefit of the righteous, but also for the seed, both the born and the unborn. "The righteous shall be in everlasting remembrance" (Ps. 112:6). Every ungodly soul mating is bondage. "Whomsoever you yield your members servant to obey, his servants ye are to whom ye obey whether of sin unto death, or of obedience unto righteousness" (Rom. 6:16).

Your seed is like the stars of the heavens. You have a brighter future and destiny that shines like the stars of the heavens. All hindrances to this commitment must be blotted out. Stones must be rolled away for angels to sit on them. No grave can swallow up your protected destiny. God separated Lot from Abraham to allow Abraham to see his destiny, the stars of blessings.

The same goes with unwholesome sexual relationships before marriage. God gave the woman caught in adultery the ability to sin no more. Without Him, we can do nothing. Jesus did not come to condemn you, man or woman engaged in this lustful relationship. He came to set you free, just like that woman. I know you desire to stop this act, but the inability to resist the urge is the problem. The God of righteousness can help you; if only you can turn to Him. Your destiny is only protected in Him.

This also applies to any other form of relationship. Some come to you just to carry out an assignment. They may present themselves to you as angels of light. When they cannot accomplish their assignments, they detach themselves with offences. Do not get disturbed. God is the one that dethrones and enthrones Kings. Any fig tree that blossoms around you may not necessary yield righteous fruit. God sees the intentions of their hearts which might not be visible to you. Some attach themselves just to see and feel what they can receive. Some are genuinely attached to you by God for just a specific time. Just be alert in the spirit to understand the reason for any relationship at a particular point in time and walk in God's divine order.

SEX OUTSIDE MARRIAGE

This abominable act is detestable to God in any relationship. This yoke interferes with God's ordained, sacred relationship. It is a spiritual taboo. It makes sense to me and to every God fearing spouse to understand why God demands a death sentence in the old covenant law for everyone caught in the act of adultery (Lev. 20:10). Thank God for his grace in Christ Jesus that is able to cover a multitude of sins. However, grace does not allow sin to abound (Rom. 6:15). "Marriage is honorable and bed undefiled. But whoremongers and adulterers God will judge" (Heb. 13:4).

Sex is a seal of trust and commitment ordained by God, and God demands it to be kept sacred and honored. Sex is the joint that connects the bones of this holy relationship, and God wants it kept holy. Once it is affected, the relationship becomes disjointed and suffers spiritual arthritis, which is pain and sorrow. Anytime there is a deviation to this sacred touch in a marital relationship, God is dishonored, and eternity is affected unless the fruit of repentance sets in, and there is a total abstinence of this abominable act of filth.

As mentioned earlier about departure from the marriage covenant, a spouse has actually departed from the loyalty of marriage when he or she engages in adultery. Furthermore, adultery is more of a danger to the soul than to the body. As stated in Prov. 6:32, "Whosoever committeth adultery with a woman lacketh understanding, he that doeth it destroyeth his own soul." God sees adultery as a destruction of the soul, which reflects His breath on earth.

Our prosperity and fulfilled life in Christ is linked up to the prosperity of our souls (3 John 1: 2). This definitely means that endangering one's soul in adultery is an easy access to poverty and death. The soul and not the spirit that sinneth shall die, but the gift of eternity is dependent on purity of mind and soul.

"Tribulation anguishes upon every soul of man that doeth evil" (Rom. 2:9). When a soul is endangered in adultery, the soul mate is affected. The soul is in danger of soul mating with an adulterous soul (Rom. 6:16). "For two shall become one flesh" (Gen. 2:24). Marriage is a submission of the bodies concerned to one another. Each flesh is glued to the other.

That soul is a servant to sin. You cannot separate your soul from your body, because man is a spirit that has a soul and lives in the body. Defying the body is defying the soul. We are encouraged "to render our bodies a living sacrifice, wholly and acceptable unto him, which is our reasonable service" (Rom. 12:1). The soul of man is God's breath on earth. God never puts His breath on any other creature He created until He created man. This breath made man a living soul. This breath activated the mortal body before man fell. Endangering our souls in adultery is defying God's breath on earth and bringing mortality to the body.

Does God hate divorce? Yes! Yet, God still approves divorce on grounds of adultery. This implies how abominable sex outside marriage is before the Lord. In other words, He considers the act disruptive to his covenant. Divorce, as a result of this misfit, could be a step to restitute the parties concerned, and marriages restored with a better understanding in both parties. "So shall thy seed be." The covenant blood ratifies relationships and makes them honorable. Fruitful and productive marriages are just like the stars of heaven.

CHAPTER 17

One Flesh: One Soul

"What? Know ye not that he which is joined to a harlot is one body with him for two," saith he, "shall become one flesh"

(1Cor. 6:16).

As mentioned earlier, a marriage covenant is soul mating. If one is involved in adultery, the danger that the sexual involvement exposes the married couple should be no surprise. This is why adultery is a gateway or entrance to evil attacks from the enemy. If a spouse becomes sexually involved with a harlot, a covenant union that involves soul mating has been created. "What! Know ye not that he that joins himself to a harlot is one body, for two shall become one flesh" (1 Cor. 6:16).

The spouse's soul is in danger of destruction, as proverbs puts it, and exposed to poverty and death including the entire family (Prov 5:8-10. Prov 6:26). Furthermore, a husband or wife sleeping with that spouse has his or her own soul in danger of death. A simple algebraic expression can explain this: A=B and B=C, then A=C. C stands for the harlot, while A and B stand for the husband and wife. If the husband and wife are one flesh and any of them is one body with a harlot, the spouse is automatically one body with the harlot as well.

A soul cannot prosper in this ungodly relationship, and a soul mate to a spouse guilty of this stands the risk of submitting to death and poverty as well. The reason is that he or she is yielding her member a servant to unrighteousness. As a result, the joy of the entire family is affected. Why? God blessed them with increase when the woman was inside the man. The man was in the image of God and not in the image of a harlot called adultery.

Our prosperity and success in life are attached to the prosperity of our souls (1John 3:2). The soul is the seat of your will and emotions that should be fed, ruled, and controlled by the Holy Spirit and the word of God in your spirit. The spouse who is guilty of this ungodly affair should rightly divide the word. Many times, we speak the word in demand of a specific need, without realizing that total submission to the Lord will direct the correct move and application of God's word.

We often seek peace in our marriage relationship and in our relationship with our kids and speak the word without a spiritual discernment of limitations to successes. The limitations could be an Achan of adultery in the relationship. As we continually submit to God, the light will surely expose the Achan in the camp of the family, and the Holy Spirit will redirect the line of prayers. Seeking his face in understanding his mind in circumstances will reframe our minds to redirect and actualize our faith in him. This is not to say that adultery is the only sin offensive to God. However, much emphasis is laid against it to obtain matrimony of peace and righteousness (Heb13:4, Matt 5:32). Appropriating the right word in a circumstance with a discernment of the root of the problem is necessary. This is not only applicable to marriages but to every situation and problems.

The correct diagnosis of every sickness brings out the correct medication. A medical prescription with wrong diagnosis may lead to death. If the earthly doctors understand this concept, how much more the kingdom giants? Christ, at this point of unfaithfulness in marriage, encouraged submission to a divorce or separation. You will now agree with me that divorce in any marital relationship starts when a spouse engages in extra-marital sexual activities and not necessarily when a judge issues a divorce certificate from the courtroom.

However, there is still room for repentance and forgiveness for any of the parties engaged in this abominable act. Therefore, a restoration of the marriage is still possible. "Blessed is every one that fears the Lord; that walketh in His ways; for thou shall eat the labor of thine hands, happy shalt thou be, and it shall be well with thee. Thy wife shall be as the fruitful vine by the sides of thine house, thy children like olive plants round about thy table" (Ps. 128:1-3). It then means to me that the productivity of a wife and the children solely depends on the fear of God in a man. God blessed them in the garden, with divine enablement to fear and love God.

The spouse and children become vulnerable to satanic attacks and forces of darkness when the spouse lives in adultery. The man may not be caught or seen cheating on his spouse, but the adverse effect and the result is seen in the lives of the wife and kids. Remember, love is not just giving worldly gifts, but protecting eternal episodes for your genealogy. Whatever we do in love and faith generates eternity. "So shall thy seed be."

What advice is necessary for a person who cheats on his/her spouse? The Grace of God is made available and sufficient to break every yoke, through his anointing. Only open yourself up to His saving grace! Eternity is in the seed.

CHAPTER 18

The Seed is Mr. Right

Who is Mr. Right or Mrs. Right? The seed is Mr. Right. Please take time and reflect on this story about a couple: Jeff and Sue were married for ten years. They lived in South Africa. The relationship faced hard times for several years. One day, they decided to hold a dialogue concerning their commitment and responsibility toward each other in their marital relationship based on their mutual understanding of the word of God; "One flesh" and "Help Meet".

JEFF: I am "Mr. Right" in the home, considering my enlightened viewpoints. Whatever I do is right. All your plans, interests, and beliefs must be in line with mine. Your finances must go through me because I have better ideas on how to run the affairs of this house financially. Moreover, I am the head of the house, and I can manage finances better than you do. Just look at things my way. "The head of the woman is the man. Man was not created for the woman, but the woman for the man" (1 Cor. 11:8-9). Your plans and preferences must be the same as mine. For us to maintain a peaceful relationship, we must not be different. God took you out of my ribs and made you exactly the way I am so we can flow and walk together, building a happy and healthy relationship. Therefore, just look at things my own way, and you will feel much better, relaxed and restful. "The head of every woman is the man and the head of the man is Christ. Man was not created for the man but the woman for the man" (1 Cor. 11:8-9). Your plans and preferences must be the same as mine, and for a peaceful relationship, we must not be different.

SUE: A "Help Meet"; sounded to me as if I were to be your helper to follow you around the world, picking up your underwear and socks, having meals ready on time, and jumping into the bed with you anytime you are in the mood. However, Jeff, I have come to realize recently that the Hebrew word for "Help Meet" is to complete you. That means I am different from you. Our plans, preferences, weak points, and strong points are different. We are never the same in our views and opinions about most issues, but we can help ourselves by realigning our differences, preferences, and priorities.

Therefore, "One flesh" and "Help meet" mean that we are here to complete each other. God brought me into your life to help you meet up and develop God's potential in you as a co-laborer to God. Jeff, you are not perfect. However, your perfection can only be seen in Christ if you come out of yourself and have a strong working relationship with the Lord through Christ. We can redirect our preferences, priorities, weak points, and strong points to Him. He will exchange all these with his own strength, ideas, and views. Christ is the 'Mr Right'

We will then stop seeing our differences and superiorities, and, instead, see His overcoming power to direct our affairs.

Child of God, marriage problems and conflicts are complex. There is no one with direct solution to these conflicts, divorces, separations, emotional and physical abuses. No one can feel your pain except the Lord. This is because if the marriage is ordained by God, it is sealed by the blood of Jesus. In that situation, He is the only one who can be touched because it affects His blood, which is His life. There is life in the blood. The truth is that the parties should learn to put their differences aside and begin to meet each other's needs. Just like SUE rightly said, Christ is the only Mr Right that can fix all differences.

There is no "Mr. Right" in any relationship except the seed that is inside of you. He is the only one that blends differences and priorities. Marriage is like two streams flowing side by side and then blending.

When the streams are together, there is a great deal of foam and splashing. However, as they become one, they are stronger and deeper than either of them individually. It does not really matter how long it takes for the blending of the two streams.

CHAPTER 19

'The' Reward and 'Not 'A' Reward

"For he that cometh to God must believe that He is and that He rewards those who diligently seek him" (Heb. 11:6). Abraham received the revelation of the reward and obeyed the rewarder. This revelation motivated him to obey God, who is the rewarder. Abraham refused to be discouraged and never disclosed his intents even to his wife but diligently sought to please the Lord. This was because he understood the reward. This understanding motivated him to offer Isaac. It is quite natural for one to be motivated to do or act right with an incentive or reward attached to obedience.

As mentioned earlier, Jesus saw the joy that was set before Him and endured the cross (Heb. 12:2). The joy was not only the empty tomb he saw before the cross but the result of the cross and empty tomb, which was the redemption of man: the innumerable souls born into the family of God or the reward of Abraham. "So shall thy seed be" as the stars of heaven, and that includes you and me. Jesus despised the manipulations of the devil. All the onslaughts of the enemy to stop His mission were bruised because of the joy that was set before Him.

THE JOY OF OBEDIENCE

Therefore, see the joy that is set before you as you pass through the waters. Beware to whom you disclose your dreams or visions, especially when it concerns doing that which seems impossible to man. You may be discouraged by so doing and, consequently, loose the blessings attached to the anticipated obedience.

Just look forward to the reward of obedience. It might look an impossible act to follow or do, and discouragement might even come from your trusted ones; however, setting your eyes on the incentive that comes with obedience will motivate your faith and trust in the Lord. I pray the Holy Spirit continuously reminds you of the incentive. This is the joy of the Lord that should actually be the strength of every believer in every pathway.

For example, God may direct you to sow $100,000, and if disclosing this information will affect your marriage negatively or discourage you from obeying the Lord, He might not want you to seek your spouse's approval, especially when both of you are not operating on the same level of faith. Even if both of you are operating in the same level of faith, be sure that disclosing this information is in God's will. In that case, the Lord will surely go before you to arrest his heart and make him/her subject and obedient to God's instructions.

Rebecca did not disclose the joy of the Lord to Isaac when the twins were in her belly. "The elder shall serve the younger." Abraham did not disclose to Sarah the intents of sacrificing Isaac, "accounting that God was able to raise him up, even from the dead; from whence also he received him in a figure" (Heb. 11:19).

Abraham saw the resurrection of Isaac in a figure. God expects our obedience at all times to be instigated by his precious promises not seen now in a figure but in Christ Jesus. Lack of divine information on these precious promises can jeopardize our willingness to obey Him. The rewarder rewards us with the reward, which is already in Christ. "All his promises are in him", "yes".

Abraham did not only see the promises, but also "he received the promises, saw them afar, was persuaded of them, embraced them, and confessed that they were strangers and pilgrims on the earth" (Heb. 11:13). The promises gave Abraham an insight of the purpose of life that he confessed with his mouth. God's promise instigates the confession we make. "So shall thy seed be."

CHAPTER 20

The Call of the Seed

Christ's ministry has its foundation or root in the call of Isaac. "By faith Abraham, when he was tried, offered up Isaac, and he that received the promises offered up his only begotten son. In Isaac shall thy seed be called" (Heb. 11:17-18). Christ's call was at the offering of Isaac.

Abrahamic covenant with God was confirmed at Mt. Moriah when he went to offer Isaac. He proclaimed the coming of the Messiah and God's purpose for his coming. "God shall provide Himself lamb for sacrifice. God saw the height of sincerity of Abraham's faith" (Gen. 22:8, 17-18), and He took over. God did not eventually provide for himself a lamb for sacrifice. Instead, He became the lamb to be offered. Abraham's offering of Isaac challenged the release of God's promise in Christ.

Our faith and obedience in offering, what to offer, and where the Lord chooses to lay the offering, provokes God for a release of His divine promises to us. Releasing the lamb at Mt. Moriah was the choice of God. God's blessings and rewards are released at the mountain of obedience. He also expects you to proclaim what you are seeing.

Elijah tagged the seed from the Zerapheth woman. Her belief in this promise instigated her obedience. Elijah was the eye of this woman (1 Kings 17:14). At times, God might send us a prophet to speak or call up our harvest through our obedience in giving. Only believe and you will see the salvation of our God.

"God so loved the world that he gave his only begotten son that whosoever believes in him, shall not perish but have everlasting life" (John 3:16). God tagged his giving. Abraham tagged his giving. God expects us always to tag our giving. Abraham's giving was not tagged by any priest; rather, God only allowed him to see and call forth his harvest on the mountain of obedience.

GIVING THAT YIELDS RESULTS

1. Give with an understanding of God's principle in giving.

    Give under God's inspiration and revelation, but not according to one's own understanding and expectations.

2. Tag your seed as the Lord directs.

    The anointing that sows is the same anointing that yields harvest. Do not sow without expecting to receive. For example, when you sow a corn seed, you expect harvest of ears of corn. The seed is called corn seed. Tagging seed and calling out expected harvest is very important.

3. Give where God directs you to give.

    "Then shall thou turn it unto money, and bind up the money in thine hand, and shall go unto the place which the Lord thy God shall choose" (Deut. 14: 25). The Lord chose Mt. Moriah for Abraham. Sow where God himself has chosen and not where man actually wants you to sow. Remember, he gives according to his riches in glory by Christ Jesus.

    He only gives, or rewards when our giving glorifies Him. Then, such giving becomes a memorial before

Him (2 Cor. 9:11-13). Our financial freedom is included in our generational package, passed from generation to generation. Our children should develop the faith in giving and learn the principles of giving as well. "So shall thy seed be.

CHAPTER 21

The Sower, The Seed, The Soil

THE SOWER

There are defined qualities of a good and acceptable sower. Some of these qualities are already described. Other qualities can be seen in 2 Cor. 8:7, "That as ye abound in every thing, in faith, and utterances, and knowledge, and in all diligence, and in your love to us, see that you abound in this grace also." Paul wished the Corinthian church would abound in a specific kind of grace, apart from grace to move mountains and for other spiritual gifts. This grace is a proof of sincerity of their love (verse 8). This is the grace of giving. Paul expects a good 'Sower' to be rich in this grace. Any act of giving void of this grace is just ceremonious. It is fleshly and not of the spirit. It is a mere unfruitful religious act. God's nature is to invest with utmost expectations of a bountiful harvest. Any act of giving void of this expectation is also fleshly. He gave life to reap lives.

What is the nature of this grace? Verse 9 has the answer: "For ye know the grace of our Lord Jesus Christ, that though he was rich, yet for your sakes, he became poor, that ye through His poverty, might be rich." The Bible calls this grace, the grace of our Lord Jesus Christ. He stripped Himself of the excellence of His glory, made Himself of no reputation for our sakes. The poverty in Christ is seen in His humility, love, generosity, and compassion. God expects us to abound richly in this grace also. "Ye, through his 'poverty'" and through this grace, we expect to be blessed and remain blessed.

Our humility, love, and compassion that accompany giving are the proofs of this grace. Our freedom is not only in material abundance we can receive but also in what we give in exchange of what we desire to receive. "He shows Himself merciful to him that is merciful, pure to him that is pure, froward to him that is froward." Likewise, "A man's life consisteth not in the abundance of things he possesses" (Luke 12:15), and "it is more blessed to give than to receive" (Acts 20:35).

This grace was rich in the Macedonian church. It is a liberating grace. This grace gives cheerfully, liberally, and with joy and satisfaction that obedience might be fulfilled. The grace releases blessings where the Lord has put His name; "… their deep poverty abounded unto the riches of their liberality" (2 Cor. 8:1-2). The Macedonian church received the revelation of this deep truth: I call this the "Grace of poverty in Christ Jesus". "For you know the grace of our Lord Jesus Christ that though He was rich, yet for your sakes He became poor, that ye through his poverty might become rich" (2Cor 8:9). Every believer is rich in Christ, but a measure of this grace in Christ Jesus generates a liberal and generous giving. That grace opened their hands to give joyfully in their deep poverty. It was not a religious or ceremonious giving but a giving that depended much on this exceeding grace in Christ. They were enriched in this grace, because they first gave themselves to the Lord.

It is not all-good works that are pleasing and fruitful but the ones enriched in this knowledge and understanding. "That ye might walk worthy of the Lord, unto all pleasing, being fruitful in every good work, and increasing in the knowledge of God" (Col. 1:10). It is the good works, motivated by this grace in Christ, that are pleasing and acceptable to God. It is not good works motivated by vain glory or seeking praise from men.

Every seed planted in and through this grace must yield bountiful harvest; otherwise, it becomes a fruitless seed. This grace first builds in compassion, love, and humility, just as in Christ Jesus. Such built in nature motivates the attitude of giving cheerfully, abundantly, and sacrificially. Do you give sacrificially or only when you are in abundance? Do you give even when your flesh is resisting it? Do you still give even when you do not feel loved? Do you still persistently give even when you feel you are not receiving, and even when the very people you give to turn round to despise and accuse you falsely? The 'Grace of poverty' should always take preeminence. Abundant and overflowing harvest comes through sacrificial giving, which I could call the 'Grace of poverty in Christ Jesus'. Moving in this grace is a demonstration of the love of God.

"So shall thy seed be."

THE SEED IS THE WORD

"In the beginning was the word, the word was with God, the word was God and the word was made flesh" (John 1:1-2). And God said, "Let us make man in our own image, after our likeness, and let them have dominion over the fish..." (Gen. 1: 26). And God blessed them, and God said "Be fruitful and multiply ..." (verse 28).

The fall of man did not change God's word, because His word is himself and remains eternal. Man only decided to hand over his dominion voluntarily to Satan. God's unchanging word brought restoration of this lost dominion to man, in person of Christ. It is only through the power in his word that this authority and dominion in man can be exercised. The word of God is God's seed on earth.

I wish to use the reproductive system in man to describe our covenant link with God. Remember, Christ loves the church and expects marriage relationship to be synonymous with his relationship with the church. The bible describes this as a mystery (Eph 5:32).

The large population of the world exists, through the sexual reproduction. At the fall of man, "Adam knew Eve, and Eve conceived and bare Cain" (Gen. 4: 1). The release of Adam's seed in Eve's ovary reproduced life. In the same way, only God's word in us brings the life changing experience. Man is reconciled to God through his word (Christ). The mating of God's word as it passes through the filopian tube of the mind, into the heart produces the victory in Christ.

The word has to be made flesh in our spirit before it can bring forth our breakthrough. The word "HOLY THING' was made flesh in the womb of Mary, through divine visitation and revelation. The heart of a regenerated man is the womb of God to conceive and bring God's prophetic plan of ruling over the planet earth, subduing the power of darkness and uplifting the overcoming victory in Christ Jesus. The word of God is the 'HOLY THING" in our hearts that must be made flesh.

"So shall thy seed be"; to rule over the vast planet, subdue kingdoms and dominions, and occupy the vast of men's heart, just like the stars are occupying the vast heavens. As we daily allow the Holy Spirit to reveal his word, we should consistently meditate on the word until the word becomes flesh in our hearts. "Then, thou shall make thy way prosperous" (Josh 1:9). "So shall thy seed be".

SOIL

"Break up your fallow ground and sow not amongst thorns" (Jer 4:3). "Sow to yourself in righteousness, reap in mercy, break up your fallow ground for it is time to seek the Lord, till he comes and rain righteousness upon you" (Hos 10:12). The soil is the heart of man. Hosea described three steps involved in sowing: Breaking up the fallow ground, seeking the Lord, and His righteousness upon one. The fertility of the heart depends on following these steps. The word of God penetrates a heart that is ready to receive, otherwise, it could fall amongst thorns and thistles, or on rocky heart, or on the sides as described in Matt 13:3-9.

The watering of every seed should be in process only when the seed penetrates the heart, otherwise, an anointing in prayer needs to first deal with the stony heart, take the veil off the eyes, so the eyes can see clearly. We should learn to understand the state of every heart before sowing a seed of increase which might be a seed of abundant harvest in health and prosperity. The increase in any area of our lives depends on the prosperity of our souls (1 John 3:1). If the heart is not ready to receive the word, then there shall be no rain or increase.

Is there any limitation in your life that needs to be broken? Limitations of offences, unforgiveness, hatred, fear, immorality fleshly lusts and desires, etc, Discovering brings forth recovering. Such limitations, when exposed by the light of the word, can be destroyed by the power of his word. "What shall it profit a man if he gains the whole world and lose his soul?"

"The word of God is quick and powerful, and sharper than any two edged sword, piercing even to the dividing asunder of the soul and the spirit, and of the joints and marrow, and is a discerner of the thoughts and intents of the heart." (Heb 4:12).

Seed sown amongst weeds gets choked up as it sprouts. Remember, the world is framed by the word (Heb 11.2). This means that the word is a frame or a container of whatever we desire. Our desire must surely be in line with God's desire. If God desires a certain limitation to be dealt with, before the release or manifestation of your own desire, he will surely wait until you ask according to his own will, according to the measure of faith that works within you, which is the faith of Jesus.

Remember, God needed a total destruction of Baal and the prophets before the outpouring of the rain. He is a God of principle. He sent the anointing in Elijah to meet face to face with Ahab the king for a total abolition of Baal in Israel (1Kings 18:1-2). The worship of Baal was a limitation to God's abundance in Israel. You may not be worshipping Baal so to say, but any form of manifestations contrary to God's word could be seen as Baal. He that revealeth the deep things of darkness can expose them, not to condemn you, but to save and deliver you.

What you might actually need at a point in time you are requesting for a perfect health, might be a perfect heart of love and forgiveness of an offender, or a perfect heart of fellowship with others. At this point in time, a healthy soul that perfects healing is needed, and asking for help to work in love, which seems impossible to the natural mind, could bring a breakthrough in your health. It could be a help to fast and intercede for others that could enlarge your coast (Is 58:7-8).

This faith cannot work outside the mind of God at any time. God desires that we keep in tune with his voice at all times. "In all thy ways, acknowledge him, and he shall direct your paths," (Prov 3:6). "This is the confidence we have, when we ask according to his will, he heareth us; and if we know that he hears us, whatsoever we ask, we know that we have the petitions that we desired of him" (1John5:14-15). The Lord hears us not just when we ask his will, but ask "according to His will". So our target in asking, is seeking His mind first. He will surely reveal it. Remember, He made darkness His secret place. Enforcing the victory in Christ Jesus by rooting out limitations through His word creates room to plant the desires of our hearts. "What ever ye shall ask in my name, that will I do, that the Father may be glorified in the Son. If ye shall ask anything in my name, I will do it" (John 14:13-14).

What does it mean to ask in His name? To ask in his name, we must first know what his name is. His name is love, acceptance, and forgiveness. His name is faithfulness. He is not only the God of miracle, but the God whose miracle is seen in His passion and love for all. So asking in his name is applying the specific and revealed name in that situation. You might have a need to ask in his 'forgiveness', forgiveness for someone else. Asking in forgiveness in that obedience opens wide the door for results (Ps130:4).

CHAPTER 22

The Mystery of God in Darkness

"He that dwells in the secret place of the most high, shall abide under the shadow of the Almighty" (Psalm 91:1). I have always prayed the Lord to give me a deep understanding of what the secret place of the Lord is. I desired not only to be in his presence but in the secret place of his presence. God is omnipresent. A revelation of his secret place has given me outstanding breakthrough in my walk with the Lord.

I had always thought that his secret place is the light of his presence, until he began to give me a deep revelation of where his secret place is, and the power that is released from his secret place. Since then, I have often desired in my life to be in the secret place, and remain there continuously.

One day, I was driving slowly behind a car, and the Lord demanded that I should carefully observe the shadow of the car moving before me, and I did. The question came to me "Can you identify the color, the make of the car, the direction of the car, from the shadow?" The answer of course was No Lord! And I heard the Spirit of the Lord say to me. "So also, the enemy cannot identify your destiny, nor your next move in my shadow". "He is not able to recognize your identity in me".

Just as my shadow moves with me, you also move with me. Shadow is produced from the reflection of light, and is most visible in darkness. "He made darkness his secret place; the pavilion round about him were dark waters and thick clouds of the skies. At the brightness that are before him, his thick clouds passed, hail stones and coals of fire" (Ps 18:11-12). "He that dwelleth in the secret place of the Most High, shall abide under the shadow of the Almighty. I will say of the Lord, He is my refuge and my fortress: my God, in him I trust." (Ps. 91:1-2). His secret place is darkness.

"To abide in" in Hebrew, is "Epimeno". This means to continue in, tarry in, indicating perseverance in continuing, whether in good or evil. The word "Dwell" in Hebrew, is "OIKEO," meaning "To inhabit as one's abode".

We are encouraged to continuously and persistently remain in the shadow of God's light or brightness, as we inhabit the secret place . In the secret place of the Lord, darkness should not bring fear, rather, joy of your position at that time should be full. This is because his most visible shadow is your refuge. God's secret place is in darkness and brightness of his presence is before him. The shadow of his light is our place of refuge and safety. We are in this shadow during trials. This is where our heavenly weapons are released. Darkness is a place of danger, confusion, uncertainty, offences and where Satan and his assigned demons raise storms of fears and intimidation. The Lord said, "This is my secret place".

You are not in the storm, God is. Do not allow the storm to affect you. Whenever you are touched or feel the impact of the storm, you have taken the position of our high priest (the Seed), that is always touched by the feelings of our infirmity, as he stays in this storm. You have switched position. Remember, darkness is his secret place. . So whenever you are faced with storms, you are in the secret place of God, positioned at his shadow for safety.

The only time you lose your joy in the storm is when you switch positions with him. Whenever you are in darkness of this world, ask him to take over that position, because it is not made for you. Your position rather, is in the shadow of his presence.

The secret place allows you to see the joy set before you. It positions you for new era of anointing and service. It positions you for a better place of fellowship and intimacy, which are all found in his shadow. Whenever you pass through any storm or difficulties, remember you are just in the Lord's secret place. It is not the time to fear. It is not the time to fret, but it is the season of wooing from the Lord. It is the most significant time in the testimony of our Lord's deliverance. It is the time to remain in the shadow, and listen to his voice. This is where the kingdom of Satan is destroyed through the hailstones, and coals of fire from his word.

You are not in the darkness. God is there. He spoke light out of darkness. The brightness of his presence goes before him. You are only sitting in the shadow of his light, unknown to the enemy. A husband seeks to woo his wife most, during the painful period of ovulation. This also attests to the greatest moment in our relationship with the Lord. It is the moment of intimacy, utmost desire for God's presence. This is the time to discover the treasures of darkness, and hidden riches in secret place unknown to the Devil. God opens and relates his secret to us during this period. Not only his secret, but also exposes the enemies intent. "He revealeth the deep and secret things, he knoweth what is in the darkness, and the light dwelleth with him" (Dan 2:22). He discovereth the deep things out of darkness (Job 12:22).

Don't seek to get out in a hurry because you might not discover all he has for you before you get out. He upholds us with his right hand of righteousness to take us through the journey. God demands we wait patiently until his work with us in this darkness is completed. It is the period of wooing. It is the period he so desires to express his intimate love. It is all about his will and not ours. It is time to seek understanding of situation and pray accordingly.

The male reproductive cell fertilizes the female ovum, and reproduces the fruit of the womb with genetic traits from both parents. So our intercourse with the Holy Spirit in his presence must definitely reproduce fruits that abound in bountiful victory. The power of the word we receive first purges and cleanses our heart. It reproves, corrects, and convinces us. "All scripture is given by inspiration of God, and is profitable for doctrine, for reprove, for correction, for instruction in righteousness: that the man of God may be thoroughly furnished unto all good works" (2 Tim3:16).

"A good man out of the good treasure of his heart brings forth that which is good and an evil man out of the evil treasure of his heart brings forth that which is evil" (Luke 6:44-45). Every fruit is known by the tree; out of the abundance of the heart, the mouth speaketh. The regenerated heart is God's womb to express his love and intimacy to mankind. Remember, fruit stays in the womb of a woman until the time of delivery. So the church of Jesus Christ as the bride is expected to conceive, bear and execute God's prophetic plan for humanity through God's word.

From the heart (womb of God), He framed the world with the fruit of his lips. He desires us to frame our world also with the fruit of our lips generated from the heart. It is, therefore, important to keep the heart pure and holy, for issues of life to flow out of it, and mould us in fiery trials. "So shall thy seed be"

CHAPTER 23

The Power in the Seed

The power of the word is in the anointing of the Holy Spirit. The anointing destroys the yoke. Why? This is because our intimacy and fellowship with God in his secret place releases tremendous anointing and boldness. You speak the word with conviction. The lord had already revealed the devices and the strategies of the devil in that darkness. He had already shown you the deep revelation of the victory of Christ in that storm.

It is no secret of what God can do, because during prayer, he had already granted you an understanding. The understanding gives you a desired knowledge and wisdom to win, because the battle is already won.

The light of his presence will expose the threats, because you are in the shadow of his presence. The anointing that penetrates the word through faith destroys the threat of darkness. The hailstones and coal of fire are symbolic of the power in the release of the revealed word. Anointing destroys the yoke that has been exposed. Jesus made an open show of the devil at the cross. Dwelling in the secret place gives us an insight into this exposure. This assists in intensifying our strength in spiritual warfare. It is important for the light of his presence to expose the threats, and the anointing in his word destroys the exposed yoke of fear, intimidations, and limitations.

BE SPECIFIC

Christians, therefore, should develop the attitude of praying specific prayers, during crisis. This means using the rhema word to speak out victory. The spirit of the word is in the rhema word. Anytime the Lord releases His rhema word in a particular situation, this word wraps the spirit or the power of release. This power of release is called the anointing. Do not deviate from this rhema word, until you see your breakthrough.

I remember sometime ago, I was being oppressed and bothered by my supervisor at work. Each time I worked into my office, I kept praying that the Lord should give me the power to submit to the authority. I thought I was praying a righteous prayer, not realizing how much this request was affecting my soul negatively. The enemy was using this request against me. One day, the Lord asked me a question that reframed my mind, and my line of prayer. The question was this: "What authority are you demanding to be submissive to?" Are you requesting for submission to the spirit of oppression, or submission to my controlling armor? This question put a puzzle and a check in my spirit. Then I realized that I was increasingly going through an intensive trauma as a result of my request. It was then that the holy Spirit revealed this scripture to me "Know ye not that to whom ye yield yourselves servants to obey, his servants ye are to whom ye obey, whether of sin unto death, or of obedience unto righteousness?" (Rom 6:16).

I realized that I am made free not only from my own sin, but also from the sin of the world. Any attack of oppression from man is a reproach of sin, and should be addressed. Man is a spirit and any oppression from man is coming from a spirit of sin and reproach. Then I realized that I had authority over my supervisor's influence on my soul, and called his soul to allign with the word of God concerning my life. Authority in the power of God's word, was to rain down fear over demonic spirit using him to oppress me. Remember, Jesus called Lazarus soul to come forth. Chains of death were broken. And Lazarus came forth.

Having received this truth, and redirecting my prayer focus, I woke up in the morning one day, and the Lord dropped this word in my

Spirit "My daughter, you will slip through his hand like a scale-less fish." This word became so real to me as I started meditating on it. I started imagining how many times a scale-less fish can slip out of our hands each time we needed to cut and prepare a meal with it. From that day, I had peace in my heart.

Few months later, I realized that his approaches towards me changed. He started being friendly that he even invited me and my family to his family's thanksgiving dinner, and a month later, he got relieved of that job. It is, therefore, necessary to pray in the spirit and let the Spirit of God that helps our infirmity identify our line of request from the Lord, so that we do not pray amiss (Rom 8: 26).

On the other hand, Jesus never prayed or thought us how to pray, with a command that we should address "every spirit", rather he said in Matt. 15:13, "That every tree my father has not planted shall be rooted out". He is not pleased when we are ignorant of the nature of the plants. Every plant or tree on the planet earth has a name. Some of them have been planted and stayed in the woods or forests for several years. Modern generation might not even know the people that planted them. Also, we may or may not have an idea of the plant responsible for every storm. It could be generational and ancestral plants, witchcraft plants, deaf and dumb plants, whoredom plants, offences and unforgiveness plants. The Lord has blotted out the handwriting of all ordinances laid against us which was contrary to us, nailing it to the cross (Col 2:14). It could also be a result of an act of disobedience, or storms to testify our growth in the Lord.

You do not invest anointing of prosperity on an unforgiving spirit that has been rooted and grounded in the heart. Whom you forgive, he forgives (2Cor 2:10). When we have grudges in our hearts, we are holding people in bondage of not receiving from the Lord, as well as ourselves. It is, therefore, most advisable to withdraw oneself from any brother or sister with offences in his heart against you, and communicate more on your knees. Thereafter, meet the brother or sister, if the Lord permits. Where there is strife and envy, there is confusion and every evil work. Offences most often could be the result of envy and jealousy. And this can create a spiritual arrow of hindrances, and limitations to great move of God in one's life. Rebecca got that revelation and set his son Jacob on an immediate journey to his brother Laban, against the offences from Esau (Gen 27:43-44).

Unforgiveness and offences plants are spiritual cancer that eat up abundance and joy in the Lord. The revealed love in Christ is needed to root the plant out first, before investing the word carrying the anointing of increase. The prosperity of soul brings the increase.

You cannot put a new wine in an old wine skin. I believe strongly in my spirit that God is much more interested in our being constantly in his presence at all times. Then and only then he will constantly reveal to us even the impending attacks from our enemy, the devil. I wish to remind us here again that before every attack, God had already given us victory. God demands we should always be on the offensive side just like Christ was, rather than on the defensive. Even before the Pharisees spoke, Christ had already known what was in their hearts. He never allowed their threats to take him unawares. Alertness in our spirits gives us insurmountable victory in Christ.

We should be able to discern when the enemy wants to attack with sickness and diseases and guide our loins with the truth of salvation and deliverance in his word and eating habits. Jesus went to the enemy's camp and took back all he took from us. We need to appropriate the reality of this act by staying on guard. More often than not, guiding our hearts diligently against all manifestations of the fruits of the flesh in Gal. 5:19; we need to arise. All undesirable plants were rooted out on the cross. (Col 2: 14).

Our breakthrough is in the renewal of our mind on the revealed word, caught up in the secret place. It is only during this time, that transformation takes place. Since God desires that we should have dominion, then we need to have a good understanding of plants and trees that have been rooted out, and apply the revealed word to enforce our victory. The specific words revealed in a specific situation or direction given in storms, are treasures in darkness. These treasures, the Lord said are hidden in earthen vessels. These treasures keep our feet strong; "troubled on every side, not distressed, perplexed, but not in despair, persecuted, but not forsaken; cast down, but not destroyed" (2Cor 4:7-9). The victory is not the physical manifestation of your expectations, but when you continually, and persistently exercise your faith in the revealed word concerning that circumstance. "This is the victory that overcometh the world, even your faith" (1 John 5: 4).

Faith in the revealed word precedes manifestations. No child is born without being made flesh in the womb. It takes the laboring in pain to put to birth. Overcoming faith is received from the revealed word made flesh in the womb of God, which is your heart. Speaking the word prophetically and believing in it is victory.

CHAPTER 24

Fruit of the Seed

Jesus said "I have chosen you ..., go into the world and bring more fruit, and that your fruit might remain". Every fruit contains a number of seeds. "Except a corn of wheat falls and dies, it abideth alone". Without the falling of a seed into the ground, and the deadness and rottenness of the seed, there shall be no fruit. Deadness of the flesh abounds in spiritual growth. Humility and brokenness is a mark of growth.

Jesus described himself as the true vine. The vine tree shoots out from the seed of the vine. We are the branches that bear the fruit, and every fruit of the vine contains multiples of the seed sown or buried. The way we live describes the tree we are attached to. God expects a reproduction of the seed in us. Ministry is, therefore, more of a reproduction and life transformation. You cannot give what you do not have. Your life transforms lives as it is transformed. You reproduce what is inside of you. Who in you makes you the who you are. The success of any ministry is measured by lives affected or changed rather than the turn out on the Sunday services. So the true vine measures the effectiveness of any ministry. This is because the true vine supplies the nourishment to the branches. The weight of fruits on the branches, causes the branches to tilt so low to allow the plucking of the fruits off the branches. Eating of these fruits by the reapers enlarges the coast of reproduction. The Lord measures the success of every ministry; not man. Success is nourishment of the house of God. A well-nourished child looks healthy, not sickly.

A good ministry is known by the victory embraced by the house. It is known by lives that have been changed, and have remained victorious. God commends and not man (2Cor12, 18). The word "ministry" in

Hebrew is 'Diakonia', meaning service, and the word "minister" means servant. The "sower" must first give himself to the Lord. Our faithfulness to God is seen in the act of giving. The chain of selfishness is broken when one sincerely and truthfully gives oneself first to the Lord. It is then and only then the true ministry emerges. No one owns a ministry, so we need to reconsider the word "my ministry" as often as we use it. "My ministry" should rather refer to our service to the Lord than our possession. Our authority is in service not in position in the church as elders or deacons or pastors and so on. "Feed the flock of God which is among you, taking the oversight thereof not by constraint but willingly … neither as being lords over God's heritage, but being examples to the flocks." (1 Peter 5: 2-3). "All things are made by him and for him are they made. In him all things consist".

Generally, lives are affected more through examples of lives we live, rather than the words we speak. Actions are more transferable than words. The ordinary words we speak are letters. Such words are not lives; they do not have the power to change our society. The word of God is spirit and life, not only spirits. "The kingdom of God is not in words but in the demonstration of the power of God" (1Cor 4:20). Jesus in the inside working on the outside; life changing in the inside, and working on the outside.

"So shall thy seed be."

CHAPTER 25

The Voice of the Seed

It is, therefore, extremely important for us all to understand the importance of creation and the redemption brought to man. We are redeemed and saved by his grace so that through the same grace, the promise to Abraham might be fulfilled in us through the promised seed of Abraham, Christ in us the hope of glory. Our salvation is not designed to just accumulate wealth and be mindful of affairs of the world and forget about the dominion over Satanic onslaughts against the soul of man. "Gain is not godliness but godliness with contentment is great gain". Riches and monetary gain are not a measure of God's abundance and blessings, but the indwelling joy and peace deposited in you every minute of the day even in storms and lightning of this world. We need to arise and occupy all the territories, guiding our minds against subtlety and evil imaginations of the kingdom of darkness to rain down sicknesses and diseases, poverty, and just like the stars of the heavens, occupy the whole vast of locations, souls in our families, places of work, every where the sole of our feet locates.

Laboring daily to enter into his rest through prayers and fasting and not being enticed by every wave of doctrine. Discovering the purpose of your salvation eliminates abuse. ARISE AND SHINE LIKE THE STARS OF THE HEAVENS!

Printed in the United States
by Baker & Taylor Publisher Services